Selling:

The Fundamentals

The enterprise sales toolbox

With love and thanks to
Carolyn, William,
Morena and Chris-
my world.

Selling: The Fundamentals

The toolkit for the enterprise Salesperson

Selling: The Fundamentals

The enterprise sales toolbox

By Marc Engall

Contents

Introduction

Introduction

Welcome to *Selling: the fundamentals*.

You've bought a toolbox of smart selling techniques. You can race through chapter by chapter, or you can dip in and simply pick out the tool as the task requires just like the master masons of old who moved from job to job.

The skill is knowing which tool to use at the right time and for how long. As any project takes shape it will change and that is when you must be ready to adapt, know when success has been reached so that you can put the tool away and select the next one.

This set of selling tools has universal application. Wherever you are in the world, regardless of language or culture, the same human instincts are at play. That is what makes your new toolbox so powerful.I want you to be able to arrive in any town or city and know how and when you can use these tools and be an outstanding success in the shortest possible time.

I have fine-tuned these techniques over 26 years of selling and they work. I regularly hit 100% of sales targets and beyond. This is where you're heading and the proof these tools work.

There are elements of science (the stone that the mason works on) and artistry (the skill that the mason develops over time) about selling. It's not so much a job that you "do," but more the person that you "become."

While selling is a process, there is an element of gutfeel and personality that each successful salesperson brings to the table. You must stick to the process, but not at the expense of human interaction and face to face engagements which require emotional intelligence, warmth, and personality. You are a salesperson when you pour in your own brand of personality and become comfortable with that over time. For some, selling is just like a project, and they become what I call "project manager-ish." There is nothing wrong with that approach as a large sale is just large project. However, not everyone is on your team, and you can't control all the moving parts on the client's side… nor for that matter your own side. So, behaving like a project manager is not the complete pathway to success.

The key to success is a blend of a structured methodology and a warm and professional personality. As in everything in life, first impressions count – if personalities clash you will hit a roadblock. But we will come to that later and show you how to adapt.

Now it is time to get going. Pick your tool and get to work. But I want to tip you off right away about one vital secret.

Selling comes first – negotiation comes last.

Read on.

1. Market Segmentation

So, you've landed your first job and let's say you're selling time management or security software. It might easily be widgets; it doesn't matter because the same challenges apply. You've been given a patch; it's the United Kingdom and the field is wide and daunting. The targets might be in the private or the public sector. Where do you begin?

A lot of people come into a selling role and don't know what to do first. You're told, "Right, you're selling security software into mobile phone companies, there's a computer, off you go! Company X is buying very little from us, chase them up!" You're in shock, do you just call up and say: "Hello, do you want to buy some more from us?" Well, maybe, maybe not.

Somehow you need to get the product or even your own business off the ground asap and get the lights on! While you might be thrilled to have your first sales job in a massive organisation, you are sitting there thinking "How do I get started? What does everyone else know that I don't? They all seem busy and have deals in the pipeline, where I have none and nobody to talk to."

You could just start at the top of the list and start cold calling, but if you manage a 1% success rate you will be doing exceptionally well. The reality is working down the list you will be here until Doomsday, and as I said at the start my aim is to get you hitting your number and beyond as soon as possible.

Step One – Prioritise size of organisation

The very first step is to break down the target list that has been dropped on your desk into priorities. You need to segment the potential targets into large, middle, and small on two dimensions:

- size of target organisation
- revenue potential to you.

Step Two – Prioritise revenue potential for your business

The next step is to analyse how well your product suits the target, you can do this in so many ways, the internet, speaking to customers of the company you are approaching, it's all good research. It is no use trying to fit a square peg into a round hole, so you can put those that don't have an immediate fit to one side. They are not discarded; they are just not right for now. Move on quickly. This is a very simple thing to do but you must start here.

What you are doing is breaking down the vast challenge into manageable blocks. If you don't do that you will be overwhelmed. Think of the mountain climber looking up at Mount Everest. It is a big challenge but not insurmountable because the climber works in stages, starting with establishing a base camp. That's where you are: preparing for the climb, establishing a safe base camp, and waiting for the right conditions.

Why bother? Why not just start climbing?

Or why not just hit the phones and start selling, taking the hits along the way because sooner or later you'll get lucky?

Prioritising is important for three reasons:

- You become focussed and avoid becoming overwhelmed and flustered
- You will gain momentum
- You will have the foundation of a plan of action, a base camp you can return to if you hit an obstacle.

Step Three – Approach

So, you have decided which of the best potential clients have the best revenue potential for your business. If any of these are existing clients already buying your products or services these are your starting point. They offer an opportunity to maintain the current revenue stream, increase the capacity (upsell) or cross-sell.

Upselling is enabling the customer to buy more of what they have already purchased from your company, and cross-selling is introducing them to some more of what you have in your portfolio.

If none of the list are existing clients, then start with the prospect that shows the best potential revenue from the biggest organisations.

Step Four - Your buckets of opportunity

You have already started to define your four buckets of opportunity. These are based on:

- The largest organisations to approach
- Best fit for your product set and therefore the organisation with the largest revenue potential in your area of interest.

Although you have now organised that daunting list of potential targets into manageable lists, they will still take you a long time to get through them all, so select the big three or four companies from your category one list and start thinking about your best approach.

Which prospective clients are the ripest? For instance, what intelligence do you have about them? Can you view strategic plans from their leadership on the organisation's website? Are they moving into new areas you can help with, or do you know someone starting a big project already? You will probably find three or four organisations that are worth approaching right away? Most importantly you have got a sound reason for making contact.

Now, you have a strategic plan, and you are ready to move from your base camp.

The rest of the large names may require a different plan. You don't know anyone working in the organisation but some of your existing partners/customers probably have a contact. Use that existing relationship to make the introduction for example: "Jane from 123.com is already working with us, she suggested that you might like to look at one of our products." You have a testimonial or solid referral. Failing that arrange for a marketing event and invite two or three of your largest best fit target companies to attend.

Step by step you work through your next levels of targets; they're smaller and should be easier to reach. Not everyone will be a winner and you will hit the occasional brick wall. But you have a strategic list so you can unplug those, put the setbacks to one side and select the next targets on your lists.

And because you have carefully segmented them there will be plenty more to approach with a reason to make contact which is very different from the random cold call.

But REMEMBER when you unplug any that you thought were best leads, you are only putting them to one side. DON'T IGNORE them leave them to mature. The next time you make contact will be a follow-up call. "Hi, Jack, you remember I called you back in January? How are things?" You are now an acquaintance, not an unknown cold caller if you take the time to record the information you found initially in your CRM system or even in your notebook.

Perhaps your conversation was not the right time for them, maybe they were working on different priorities or there was no budget. Some might even come back to you in six months' time and say: "You were talking to us about your product earlier, well now we have some budget. Can we talk again?" so they move back to the top of your list. You have a rolling portfolio of prospective clients -in various stages of your segmentation approach. This is a constantly shifting but focussed process. Avoid spending the entire year on a single prospective Client because you will be missing out other potentials that could be fruitful, the skill is placing bets with your time.

Some salespeople have only one large prospect, you may be thinking there is no opportunity for segmentation, however you can still apply a segmentation process to this potential client based on size of department and revenue potential for you.

Let's look a little more closely about using the RESOURCES you have at your disposal which when you first arrived on the job you were totally unaware of or were too nervous to ask about.

I have already mentioned existing customers who could provide an introduction. But let's say you have no easy connection like that. Maybe you know of someone through LinkedIn who has moved into a role at an organisation you are targeting.

First, check all the data you have internally on that target, then what's in the public domain and have they recently issued any Invitation to Tenders (ITT) or hired people that you suspect may have interest in talking to you. Then you make your first call from an informed position because you know that your product is a potential fit and it may be the right time for them to buy.

Your strategy with an existing client if you are seeking upsell or cross sell may be just to be bold, put in a call and ask someone that is familiar with your company: If I were to approach someone in your company who would that be? They may give you a name. Then you look this lead up on LinkedIn and set up a meeting with them. You have a better chance of this because they have been introduced by one of their own colleagues.

Alternatively, you could ask one of your partners/existing customers if they know anyone in your target companies perhaps because they are already selling to them or have worked with them in the past. Do you think they are good customers; might they be a good fit for your product? Can you set up a meeting for me? Now when you speak with the prospect you have a name; you have a mutual contact/friend and that vital first impression is warmer. You are no longer just a salesperson but a contact of someone they are already doing good business with and therefore think you are probably a reliable introduction.

Hitting an unclimbable sheer cliff face

What happens when you really run up against an unclimbable cliff face in one of these conversations and you get a flat out no? What you do is go back to the start of the process, choose another target, and try again. You always try again.

Another approach is to try a completely different tack. You should put a message up on your own company internal messaging system to find out if anyone has a contact in one of your target companies. Do the same with your partners/existing clients because there is always one person with a contact. These are big companies with thousands of employees and no doubt hundreds at a senior level. Remember the theory of six degrees of separation: Someone will always know someone somewhere.

Let's recap. Market Segmentation is about targeting your priorities: breaking down the task into manageable and logical steps.

In segmenting your market, you should research your top five or ten targets from internal and public domain sources. That takes time but it's essential. A handy hint - set up a Google alert for companies you're interested in, and Google will send you daily news stories about these companies.

These alerts may throw up the name of someone with a problem they are trying to sort out in your field. Your next steps should be:

a) Can you contact that person directly?

b) Is there someone in your company that knows this person

c) Is there a partner/existing client you are already working with who might have a link?

Now you have a target point in that company one specific person rather than 20,000 faceless, nameless people. Your goal is to connect with an executive in the company who may become your sponsor on the inside.

Action list: your next steps

- **Segment** – break down your list of targets into separate lists according to size, fit and potential revenue for you. The problem is no longer insurmountable, and it demonstrates that you have a plan of action.
- **Prioritise** – you have established your base camp for the climb ahead –You can't tackle the whole mountain in one assault so prioritise into these buckets and start working on the best potentials first.
- **Research & Resources** – to fine tune these categories require research. There is public information on the Internet but don't forget your own internal resources. Internal messaging might provide that vital introduction. Approach existing clients/partners to see if they have a contact who can help and don't forget the tip on Google alerts.
- **Try Again** – not every answer will be yes, but not every answer is a definite no. It maybe "not yet" for a variety of reasons: no budget, or simply wrong timing. Set aside that target but don't forget them. Always try again.

Resources

www.salesforce.com

www.hoovers.com

www.discoverorg.com

2. Salespeople and Field Marketing

Salespeople and marketers are two sides of the same coin. One cannot exist without the other and yet there is often a conflict. It's not a competition. It's not a battle to see who comes out on top.

Field marketers are a specialist bunch of marketing people whose objectives are to generate demand and create leads for salespeople who are likely to become customers.

Why is field marketing so important?

Simply stated, Field marketers establish initial interest in your company's product or services before salespeople get involved.

To be able to understand the customers intentions at a greater level of detail you need people closest to the customer and you can't do that if you're sitting in market research back in head office. You need people in the field speaking the same language and have enough people to be able to be close to the customer.

In a small company your sales team may also act as marketers. A larger organisation might have may field marketing roles: market research, web marketing, search engine optimisation and campaign managers.

Marketing is necessary in all stages of the buyer's journey. Equally feedback from the sales team keeps the marketing effort in touch with current trends.

There is an adage: "If you do what you have always done, you get what you've always got." The market is constantly changing – and you need to change your approach to keep pace, doing what you have always done may no longer work.

Sales & Marketing tools

There's an ocean of tools out there for the salesperson and the Marketeers both of whom need to work together to achieve the best outcome. Sales and Marketing people will choose particular tools based on objectives and tactics.

For example:

- You might run regional campaigns. Web localisation will offer pages that reflect your message to each region.
- You would need a database to execute some account-based marketing.

You can execute campaigns more effectively if you have correct tools that give you insights around potential client's likelihood to buy sometimes called Account Based Marketing. Typically, you would need marketing tools that are plugged into a broader Customer Relationship Management (CRM) tool which is the beating heart of the sales and marketing organisation.

Essentially, the point of the tools is to deliver tailored messages to a set of potential clients. Then you can qualify their intention to buy and, this maybe a good place to start a conversation or rule that contact out for the time being.

Crucially you must manage your resources enabling you to quickly measure your results and adapt your activities so that you can react to things that are happening locally.

How should the salesperson work with the field marketing people?

Respectfully!

You must start by understanding and accepting a couple of points. Field marketing and sales must collaborate and only together can you determine what marketing strategies will have a high success rate. But that said you must respect each other's specialisms. The field marketer wouldn't tell the salesperson how to close a deal, nor would the salesperson tell a marketing expert how to run an event.

Working together effectively involves finding find out each other's objectives and targets, if your motivations are not aligned then you're going to struggle to work together.

There is always finite resources and budget in a field marketing team, your challenge as a salesperson is to understand how much of that resource and budget can be applied for your benefit. You must be creative for instance can you piggyback off other campaigns? Can you squeeze a bit extra out of a budget? Can you reuse some collateral?

Just be completely open and transparent about your respective resources. For instance, a positive way is to ask if the marketing team will present to you and you present back to them, so everyone understands their role, their strategy, and their resources.

Basic Principles

The number one cause of friction between sales and marketing relates to the quality and quantity of leads

Seasoned salespeople understand that success it is about running a successful sales cycle that closes. The successful sales operators think about their area as a franchise using the resources of the wider business-like marketing to help them in their task. It's not a competitive task in terms of creating more leads than marketing, and if you align properly and communicate effectively with the wider team you can expect their support and help as you move forward. This approach offers the maximum benefit, you have everything to gain and little to lose.

Marketing can spend a large chunk of their budget developing a prospect before handing it over to sales who close the deal with much back slapping. Remember to celebrate with everyone who was involved.

Feedback

One of the most effective ways to strengthen that link is to hold regular sales and marketing meetings to share your plans and insights.

By simply explaining how you were talking to a potential lead about their needs, is valuable to the marketing team who can develop that into messaging and marketing campaigns.

Regular face to face meetings are important as everyone begins to feel part of the same team. It should become non-competitive and non-confrontational.

If a campaign has not gone well there should be a free and open discussion to analyse why and how tactics can be changed for the better. Its an open discussion round the table with everyone including marketing, pre-sales and sales in what becomes a regular review. Maybe the leads were not great quality and there can be a frank discussion as to why not. When it is approached in the right way, in a safe environment, much can be achieved. Above all there is no anger and no finger pointing it's a team approach.

What you are aiming for is a strategy to improve what might even have been a successful campaign. So, you analyse every aspect good and bad, you are taking the "outcome" out of the discussion. It doesn't matter whether or not the campaign was a success, and you landed a major client. You should be asking yourself and the team how we could have done better? Win or lose, focus on the performance regardless of success. It is the relentless, unforgiving path to achieving sales figures we promised ourselves at the start of this book.

It's not about speed of leads, it's about the value

This follows directly from the last point. The volume of leads is something that many salespeople and marketers both strive to increase, but this should never be at the expense of the lead quality.

Often volume and quality are undoubtedly linked; but filling the sales team with volume at the expense of all else just creates busy fools.

At what point volume reduces quality will vary from business to business, and from the type of activities you carry out to achieve higher levels of volume and should be carefully and regularly monitored by conversion rates.

Marketing can help massively in determining the highest value segments depending on the data available enabling the team to assess the potential and intent of the customers.

Then when it comes to launching a campaign, it is no good just reaching for the standard package you have always used or indeed passing the task to marketing and expecting them to come up with all the ideas, its your business and you need to have a "paddle in the water". Make sure you work as a team, sitting together with local pre-sales, sales and marketing right from the start to create a proposition that will resonate with the target audience.

Summary

- **Sales & Marketing** - you're on the same side, there is no competition and work as a team, you are on the same side
- **Why is marketing so important?** – to keep the engine of your business fuelled with new leads and opportunities
- **Tools of the Trade** – see Resources below
- **How should the salesperson approach field marketing?** - Respectfully! And with ideas for campaigns in your area
- **Basic Principles** – friction between sales and marketing can occur for a variety of reasons but the number one is the source and quality of leads
- **Feedback** - hold weekly sales and marketing meetings to make the good campaigns even better
- **It's not about speed of leads, it's about the value** - the point at which volume reduces quality
- **The Covid Effect** – the world and deal-making are moving faster; sales and marketing will need to adapt.

Resources –

www.hubspot.com

www.marketo.com

www.salesforce.com

3. Social Selling

You are not alone. So why do so many salespeople act as though they are?

Some statistics suggest that 75% of you are not taking advantage of the power of social selling. Even if it is only 50%, that is still a lot of potential going to waste since most B2B decision makers use social media to do their research.

It has transformed my operating methods, now it is time to change yours for the better.

What is social selling? Social selling is selling via communities on the Internet using platforms like LinkedIn, Facebook and Instagram. The best news is that there are countless millions of subscribers who sign up for free and upload their profiles and other valuable information. Valuable to you.

It gives you market insight into what's currently important to individuals and companies. It helps you understand new trends and importantly understand what your competition is doing.

First steps
The first thing to do is ensure you have a presence as a salesperson on these platforms and to ensure the company you work for has a presence too. My preference and yours should be LinkedIn which is much more business related. Facebook and Instagram are more about people's personal lives and interests, whereas LinkedIn is about your professional life and business transactions making it the largest and most important B2B social selling platform, although the others like Twitter should not be forgotten.

Content is everything

Your influence will only go so far with certain content so beware.

There are two types of content that can be put on these platforms: the first is news about your own company and the second is stories or insights you have written about the market.

Constantly writing about/promoting your own company and its products is like a television channel that only plays advertisements from one company. It's dull and will soon lose viewers. You will quickly find this turns into an echo chamber where the only people liking, and commenting are other people from your company reflecting at you. Far better to talk about market trends that your company is involved in because that is adding to the intellectual gene pool of your feed and subscribers will keep logging in to see what else they can learn from you about your market.

As a rule of thumb, I would suggest one post about your company for every four or five about the sector you are following. From a salesperson's point of view, you need to understand that what you say gets looked at for a brief second or two and it will very quickly be scrolled over if all it amounts to is yet another plug for your company.

The Power of Groups

What you are attempting to do is capture the interest of as many people as possible in your target area of interest and the easiest, and often neglected, way of doing this is setting up Linkedin groups. For example, you may be involved in TV broadcast security so you would send out invitations to people you already know, or you have a distant connection with, and invite them to read a background article you have written on the subject.

All the other person has to do is tick a box saying they are interested. It requires no more effort from them, but a firmer connection has been established between you both. You may only have met briefly via the Internet before, but it opens the door for a follow up.

Once they're in your group you or your Business Development Rep can then take the leap and give them a call or send an email and say: "Thanks for joining the group, this is what the group's all about it's talking about security and broadcast technology, I understand that's what you do. I wondered if you'd be happy to have a conversation for five minutes." That's another way of bridging the gap so when you do make that call if they accept and say: "Yes, let's have a chat on Tuesday morning at 10" the conversation is much easier. That makes it a warm call as opposed to a cold call. They're expecting to hear from you, they know what it's about and they have scheduled a meeting in their diary as a result you'll get a much better response. Just to call someone up that you have tracked down on the Internet is weak, but to be able to say that you have noted their interest in a feature you have posted in your group is more powerful making it a much stronger connection. In social terms you are starting a conversation.

Your company might decide it wants to host an event. This where the concept of safety in numbers applies. Consider the difference between inviting someone to a one-on-one meeting and the prospect of a gathering of like-minded people with a mutual interest. For the potential client it seems easier, not to mention the chance of finding out more information about what is happening in their sector from other guests. The response to the invitation to an event you have trailed in earlier posts is much more likely to be positive.

Steppingstones to trust

I view social selling as being like a bank account. If all you do is withdraw from the account instead of investing, then the account will very soon run dry, and it will be closed. Similarly, with your contacts and your groups. It is all about steppingstones to build up that trust, that interest, over time, and it should be a continuous process.

Once you establish a connection and you know there is a mutual interest, it is like any friendship it needs to be nurtured, feeding the account. You cannot always be making withdrawals, expecting your contacts to buy every time you have something to sell. You have to say that this relationship between you is going to be valuable over time and so you're going to post this useful information to them and down the line ask for a 10-minute meeting or a 5-minute call which you know is hugely outweighed by the valuable information that you have already shared with them. By posting regularly and intelligently you are ensuring that your company and product will become "front of mind" to your contacts; they will automatically think of you when it comes to making their next purchase.

Social selling has transformed the traditional selling process moving away from the petrifying, tough cold call where the phone weighs a hundred tonnes every time you pick it up to dial another number. Let's face it there was a huge amount of hesitance and failure there. These days technology has allowed machines to make many of those calls in the B2C sector although I'm not convinced it works that well. The difference with social selling is the jumping off point is sending out 20 or 30 invitations to people who have a similar interest before making the call and the technology exists to send out multiple invitations designed for a particular audience, be it LinkedIn, Facebook, Twitter or Instagram all at the same time.

Some of these platforms also have deeper selling tools for you to use which enable you to monitor a particular contact, see what they're doing, if they're changing jobs and what they themselves are posting. It allows you to organise your time better and strike at the right time for the potential client.

Risks and opportunities
Remember you are dealing with a potentially vast audience which means there are both risks and opportunities in social selling. For example, you may have gleaned some internal information from the marketing department about a new product which is about to be launched but you inadvertently jump the gun and post it on one of your groups. As a result, not just one but potentially hundreds if not thousands of people now know all about it.

So never write and post anything you wouldn't want said in public because not just one business associate, but your entire network will be able to read all about it. And by connection all their contacts will have that same confidential data which may be something incendiary like a profit warning that's coming out ahead of the market or you're divesting a company or buying another.

On the other hand, there are fantastic opportunities not only in terms of the speed but also the reach of these online platforms. When I say you are not alone, I mean your potential audiences may run into the tens of thousands when you launch your latest product. Your news/your advertisement can be viewed globally, 24/7 in an instant, in full colour with video and it's free. That's the reward side of social selling.

You can think of it as another element of traditional advertising, which is facing severe competition from the online market. Newspaper and magazine advertising in the United States, for example, is forecast to fall by 2024 to a total of $5.5 billion from $25 billion in 2012, according to Global Media forecasters, GroupM (www.groupm.com)

Getting a wider audience

Once you have established your presence on your chosen platform, your first task is to maximise your audience and then, crucially, to keep them interested and involved.

Content is key and you should chase your marketing department for news which you upload on a regular, even daily, basis. Keep abreast of what is being discussed in your industry magazines, post your opinion and invite your group to comment which could simply be clicking on a Like/Disagree button, which is good for both of you as you don't want to spend six months pursuing a prospect with no interest in your company, and you don't lose favour with them by pestering them with phone calls.

Remember you are trying to maintain a conversation so the next time you make a direct call after a Linkedin chat it is a warm call; you are making a personal link with more and more people, drawing them into the discussion. It is an ongoing, constant task to keep building your network.

The purpose of your posts is to get a positive reaction which means you now have a good reason to call, and it is pertinent to them which increases your odds 100% of achieving a sale.

So how do you move from an online conversation to a more substantial meeting?

For example, let's say John is now a member of your group and he has liked some of your posts about your software. He becomes a good potential target because at the very least he is interested in your market. You then make contact via LinkedIn's internal messages "Inmails" you ask John if he is interested in the topic and would like to chat further? If you get a positive response from John and depending on the size of your company. You either give that lead to one of your business developments people to make the phone call or you make the call yourself

You might say: "I notice we're in the same group thanks for the connection. Glad we're talking about the same things; would you like to have a conversation about our software? Where are you on your journey in implementing this type of software? Have you got any software solutions in mind that you have seen in the market? Have you talked to anyone else?"

These are just a few opening questions that you can use that will start the conversation or will shut it down. Your target might say: "I really don't have time for this" or "That's interesting, I've never really considered your company for this type of thing".

That's where you start to engage directly. If you get a positive response you could follow up with: "If this is interesting to you then maybe, we can set up a longer meeting. I know I've kind of pounced on you today but we can schedule another meeting when I can talk with you about what we've done for other clients, and we maybe can have a technical demo so we can run you through the product and you can actually see it working. What about tomorrow or next week?"

And that's where you have the face-to-face meeting or these days a video call, and you would invite your sales engineer or solutions engineer who is a technical person to demonstrate the product making it sing and dance. Hopefully, that will entice them to look more closely at the product and then maybe go into a deeper investigation with their own team.

Ideally you want to be able to show them reference cases of your success stories where you were able to save a company a great deal of money or where they had some other issue. Your company came in, installed your software and over a period of time solved their problem.

Why not just send an email? The problem is that 99 times out of 100 that email will not get read or it will go straight into Trash or spam. Platforms like LinkedIn are more personal and probably wouldn't be read during the working day. It is more likely to be opened at the weekend, in the evening or on the train home. It gets above the 'noise' of other messages and usually it is shorter, probably two paragraphs at the most, and it goes directly to your contact, not filtered by a PA.

You are now the CEO
Congratulations! You are now the CEO of your own franchise, at least that is the way I see the role of the successful salesperson. Just like the leader of a small team on a mountain, you are in-control, of the actions of the team and certainly the direction.

Depending on the size of the company you have many valuable resources at your disposal and they're mostly free (with a few exceptions like Linkedin Navigator an add-on tool to help you). Not only are they free but, in effect, they are working for you or can be made to work for you.

You are most certainly not alone because you have the Marketing Department and the Business Development specialists. They are all producing data, information, releases, and background analyses, so why not use that material in your posts – remember it is valuable and it is FREE? This is where you put your franchise hat on. You have become the CEO of your own operation.

What I try and do is ensure I get more than my fair share of the support from every company department. I constantly chase them for news, their opinions, and their output. And I make suggestions to them: Do you think we could hold an event about such and such? Then I immediately post stories about that forthcoming event and send out invitations.

The marketing department may well be putting up posts to their own network – become part of it and thereby expand your own reach. In the same way the marketing department will love it because they can extend their reach into your network which in turn will produce new leads.

So, work with marketing and business development and the chances are they will welcome your interest in their activity because all too often they work in isolation not utilising sales as a valuable resource for them.
Instead of joining a company and being terrified that you are on your own, actually you have acquired all this amazing, FREE, resource just waiting to help you out. They are now part of YOUR team.

What you must develop is the mindset that you are the BOSS of your own world and reach out to harness those assets. Don't become blinkered and must narrow a focus feeling you have got to put out another post but struggling to think what to say.

Every company will be planning ahead perhaps with a new launch or a marketing drive or be scheduling a major event. These are all gold dust to the salesperson and your ever-expanding group.

In my experience these valuable resources which are all available to you will fall over themselves if you just show some interest in them because they are chasing customers too. If you fail to reach out and fail to ask their opinions, then you are missing a huge opportunity. You are a sales expert; you know how to ask questions so search out and meet all the consultants and highly paid advisers who may be already employed by your company and tap into their output. All your Christmas' and Birthdays have come at once and your own franchise, the business you are running by yourself, suddenly has a team of employees who are all working for you to help you succeed.

Summary

- **Create an Linkedin/Twitter presence** – the first step in social selling
- **Build a group** – to maximise your audience and spread your news
- **Content is everything -** there are two types of content that can be put on Internet platforms: the first is news about your own company and the second is stories or insights you have written about the sector
- **Beware the risks - exploit the opportunities** – you are not alone on the Internet so beware what you share, its there for ever
- **Use your free inhouse resources -** you have many valuable resources at your disposal and they're all free. Not only are they free but, in effect, they are working for you or can be made to work for you
- **You are your own CEO -** develop the mindset that you are the BOSS of your own world and reach out to harness the assets at your fingertips.

Resources:
www.linkedin.com
Linkedin Sales Navigator
https://maverrik.io

33

4.Managing yourself

Time and tide wait for no man, as the proverb says, so what are you waiting for?

You cannot manage time: it ticks away relentlessly, regardless of what you plan or do. Time is the most precious commodity you have, once lost it is gone forever. You won't even get back the time it takes to read this, no matter how hard you try or how wealthy you become. The most important skill to acquire is 'the management of yourself rather than the management of time'. And you can do this by taking control of your day. After all, who else is in charge, if not you?

Taking control may be as simple as managing your email inbox, handling a non-urgent phone call, the TV show you can't miss, making another coffee, or even thinking about what you really need to be doing today.

Now, more than ever, you are a target for distraction. You may be searching the Internet for some fact to put in a report and, before you know it, you have been led off on a tangent by something that has popped up on your screen – yet another email, a text message, or a compelling advert. Or you might experience the "why on earth did I pick up my phone?" moment. Not surprisingly, it's sometimes called "WILF-ing" (What Was I Looking For?)

Distraction – It's not your fault

Let's just agree we live in a distracting world, and productivity suffers absolutely as a result. But ask yourself: when you open your email inbox, is that **YOUR** to-do-list or someone else's?

Avoid the wrong mindset

The minute you open your email inbox, it's almost impossible to avoid reading all your mail. Afterwards you will certainly feel like you have completed at least one task already that day. Then you can make a to-do-list based on your inbox, or, worse, you simply answer each email in turn: It's virtually impossible to avoid following such a distracting routine because every time you complete tasks such as responding to an email or putting it on a list, there's a release of dopamine in your brain that feels like a little reward. How does that suggest you are taking control of **YOUR** day by focussing on **YOUR** tasks? It's clearly not.

You can think of your available time as a leaky bucket. You can choose which leaks to plug or you can ignore all the leaks. However, simply by prioritising your activities will mean you're always focused on the most important tasks that will make you and your leadership team very happy.

And there's a very simple way to get started – all it requires is a pencil and a piece of paper.

A reliable remedy for information overload

Take an A4 piece of plain paper, fold it in half then half again so you have an A6 sized booklet that will fit neatly into your pocket (roughly 11cm x 15cm).

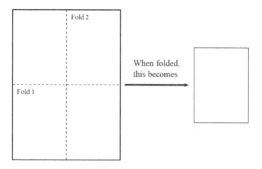

On Sunday evening, sit down with your favourite drink or snack (you do need to be disciplined about being good to yourself too) and take out your booklet.

In the first section (any will do), write down all the things you want to accomplish that week. Include:

- accomplishments in your private life (maybe taking the dog to the vet, booking the car in for a service or picking up a Mother's Day treat), and
- accomplishments that are important on a tactical or strategic level in your job. Include items such as finding out who is the buyer in a target organisation or making time to reach ten prospects each day (turning off your email is a good place to start).

Still on Sunday, write down in the next section what you hope to accomplish on Monday, carved from the overall weekly list. These two lists should take you no more than 30 minutes to write.

You may have guessed already what you need to do on Monday evening as you close down for the day. Yes, you turn to the next section and write down Tuesday's effort toward your weekly accomplishments. If you didn't manage to achieve all of Monday's list, that's fine. Simply add outstanding items to Tuesday or Wednesday, but don't lose sight of them. And you can use the other side of the booklet for the remaining days of the week.

Nothing gets in the way of your **paper** list. If you try to carry out the same exercise on your mobile phone you will very quickly get distracted by other things on the screen.

If you have more items that flow in during the week, simply add them to a day that feels appropriate and add them to the weekly list, too. This is partly why a booklet is better use than a book: it's difficult to put a book into your pocket and get out when you suddenly have an idea on the move or remember something you must do this week.

This approach helps you to understand the following:
- What you must do this week
- What you must do today
- What didn't get done yesterday
- What you achieved this week (and whether it was a good week).

There's a bonus - it will also help you sleep better, safe in the knowledge that your day is planned, and you know from the moment you wake up you're on-track.

I will admit to a sad and guilty secret - I also use this booklet at the weekends for remembering chores like buying wood at the DIY store and cleaning up the garage so I can work on my bikes.

Be Flexible

And now you may be wondering how this booklet helps with what to do in a sales cycle.

There are people who would have you focusing on all the stages of the sales cycle all the time and pushing every single client all the time in the vain hope that this will create more sales. Don't let such people set your agenda. Their approach is confusing, because none of us can genuinely multitask effectively, regardless of IQ or gender. Also, trying to multitask makes you less effective at all the tasks you undertake. (See the link in the resources at the end of this chapter which supports this claim: "multi-tasking reduces your IQ".)

Stay flexible but do not ignore voicemails or emails. Keep up to date at set times and return calls at least twice a day, but don't be a slave to others. Even the best communications plans survive only until you meet the reality of the day's events; you may have bumps along the way, and you may not complete any of your planned goals, but your daily review will highlight your progress (or lack of progress). Therefore, you need to allocate time to pick up again your incomplete tasks rather than allow other people's defined tasks to set your pace. If you sometimes fall off the wagon of this discipline (and everyone does at some point), don't beat yourself up – at least you have a wagon to climb back on to.

Remember the words of Helmuth von Moltke the Elder, the Prussian field marshal, popularly translated as:

"No plan survives first contact with the enemy."

Or, in the words of the boxer Mike Tyson:

"Everyone has a plan until they get punched in the mouth.

For us, that means:

"No business plan survives first contact with the customer."

However, this is not a danger for you because you have a flexible campaign strategy. You won't be firing in all directions but taking decisive steps in the direction you choose.

Now's the time to turn to General Dwight D. Eisenhower.

He is credited with creating the Eisenhower matrix. This can help guide you in the pursuit of what to do next.

Here's how it works:

Important stuff is what helps you achieve your goals. Important stuff is important **to you**, helping you make progress rather than just putting you back into a state you've
been in before. Urgent stuff **for you** has a deadline, after which it's not worth doing. For instance, putting out a fire could well be an urgent task for

you. Aim to be doing now only important, urgent tasks or taking time out to do the important tasks that have no deadline - these are important to you, though others may not share your view. Everything else needs to wait it's turn, go to someone else's task list or be eliminated from your day. Applying this approach is not easy and requires a paradigm shift in thinking, but, if you start going about things in this way, you will achieve more of the important stuff and be less bogged-down with things that "don't make the boat go faster" (in the words of Ben Hunt-Davis, the Olympic gold medal winner in rowing).

What do you do when you don't know what to do?
Let's return to our booklet, our folded piece of paper. This isn't just an *aide memoire*:
• It is a never-ending pipeline of ideas that you refill every day.

At the start of your time in sales, you'll spend almost 100% of your day prospecting: finding opportunities to work on. These opportunities are **"new"**. You'll also get some opportunities that will need some time to develop but won't close in the current quarter. The opportunities are **"in the pipeline"**. Finally, you'll have a handful of deals that you have a high likelihood of closing this quarter. These opportunities are **"most likely"**.

The common but less successful way of approaching opportunities at different stages of development is to work equally on each of them at the same time. The trouble is that this creates a sine wave of activity compared to outcome rising and falling regardless of the effort you put in.

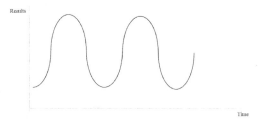

Results

Time

Initially, you'll spend your time in **new**, then **in the pipeline** and then then in **most likely**. This begs the question, "When do you go back to creating **new** again?" The typical answer is when your pipeline is empty, and people in your organisation are screaming for more business. Then the cycle repeats.

Instead, you should organise your efforts in this way according to Miller Heiman in their Strategic Selling book:

1)   **Most likely** - this is where you focus on all the activities you can accomplish with the client each day. You've got your deals that are highly likely to close:

- You have taken the prospects through the pipeline
- You've done your demo and they are happy
- they've got the paperwork and
- you think they're going to order this month or this quarter.

That's what is called **Most Likely.** Then you will be waiting for responses either internally or from the client.

While you're waiting is a perfect time to focus on **new**.

2)   **New** - this is about creating new beginnings.

- This stage includes calling, emailing, social selling, researching, talking with partners, and going to new meetings.

3)   **In the pipeline** – this is about moving forward with opportunities.

- You have spoken to somebody; you've got them engaged, and they want to talk to you. These are the opportunities that are **in the pipeline**. You should get on with this set of your pipeline and do the things that will move you closer to winning the deals in future quarters.

This way of prioritising your days will mean:

- You are always focussed on the most important tasks, which will make you feel the progress you are making and keep your leadership team very happy
- You will never run out of **new** prospects in your pipeline. If you do, it's immediately obvious so you can change tack or get help.
- You are consistently working on your pipeline to bring each opportunity closer to a signed deal.

Think of your pipeline rising when a **"new"** is fed in, then falling when sales are closed.

When new prospects are being fed into the pipeline all the time, you are never asking yourself: "What should I do next?"

The alternative to this way of working is a sales cycle that ebbs and flows, beginning with lots of activity but not a great deal of prospecting because you're busy working on closing deals. But, when you close these deals, your pipeline is empty, and you must start at the beginning again.

Remember, always put your primary focus on the "most likely" deals that will make you and your leadership team happy because these deals will also be a focused of attention. Then feed the pipeline, closing the business you can see in front of you and building new prospects.

A word of caution…

Some people may not appreciate this approach to pipeline management and self-management. You might have a manager who insists on your responding to their every instruction immediately. In this case, feeding into the pipeline AND filtering out the not important tasks (for you) might alienate you from them. It's important to apply your effort in a phased way and over several weeks or months. Try to block out time in your diary rather than just turning off your email. Treat the time you spend on these stages like a meeting with yourself. The purpose of these meetings is to focus separately on the most likely, the new and opportunities that are in the pipeline.

If you just think about things in this way and act accordingly, you'll be more effective. You will complete the tasks that you have for yourself while also impressing others in your business that you make time for the important stuff and that you deliver.

Summary
- **Take control of your day** – accept that you live in a distracting world.
- **Decide who is charge?** – don't let your emails set the agenda for your day.
- **Manage your leaky bucket** – choose which leaks to plug and which to ignore.
- **Apply the folded paper and pencil technique** – a simple method to plan your week and keep you on track.

- **Keep filling the pipeline** – this is the best way to find new opportunities AND keep you and your management team happy.
- **Be flexible** – you cannot focus on your most likely leads all the time. Remember to keep the rest of your pipeline moving forward.
- **Apply the Eisenhower Matrix** – some things are important and urgent for you; but schedule time for things that are just important. Otherwise, they'll never get done, and you won't make the progress you want.

Resources:
https://www.millerheimangroup.academy/en/
Multi-tasking reduces your IQ:

5.Face to Face

The day finally arrives when you must have your first face-to-face meeting with a prospective customer. Your nerves are jangling, and tension is high. You may have had some telephone discussions, but this will be different.

It's an age old saying but true all the same: "You never get a second opportunity to make a first impression."

First impression
My first rule is **don't be late**. Punctuality is paramount because if you keep the client waiting, you're already failing before you have even walked in the door.I always aim to get to a meeting ten minutes early. Anything more than that and I ask the receptionist to let my counterpart know I have arrived, but to say I am happy to wait, which leaves the option to start early if that suits them.

You've got to make yourself user-friendly to the broadest possible audience because you never know what the person on the other side of the table is going to feel about you or how they going to behave:

- Some people are incredibly formal
- Some people are very relaxed
- Some people inject humour and others are serious.

You must be what I call 'a social chameleon,' matching their moods, mirroring their actions. If they lean forward, you lean forward if they fold their arms, you fold your arms. It's a technique for establishing a small connection and rapport.

I'm not talking about being contrived or mimicking the other person but ensuring that you do not become the centre of attention because of your appearance or your behaviour. **The product or the service you are selling is all that matters.**

Remember, people make up their minds about you in the first seconds you walk into a room. They will judge you on your clothes, on your hair, on your manners, even before you have uttered a word.

In a face-to-face encounter, how you look matters hugely and can be perfected with ease by ensuring your hair is tidy, your clothes fit, and your shoes are clean. What you actually wear - smart casual or formal - depends entirely on whom you are meeting – the biggest challenge for men, at least these days, is deciding whether or not to wear a tie!

If the only thing the client remembers is that you wore a brightly coloured, loud tie or you wore pink socks and kept referring to them, it will detract from why you were there in the first place.

The Greeting

Whether you are meeting a man or a woman, all you need is a good handshake which should be firm but not crushing.

Then there's the somewhat awkward march to the meeting room – do you strike up a conversation about the weather or walk in polite silence? You could resort to **F.O.R.M: Family, Occupation, Recreation and Money**. Pretty much everyone in the business world will have an opinion or viewpoint on such a list of subjects, so it's worthwhile scanning the headlines on your way to the meeting so you have something in mind in case you need to create conversation.

Be Prepared

I will assume that you know your own business well enough to make a presentation, but what do you know about the customer?

Before your appointment, research their company and their industry, read their board messages and papers if they are in the public domain and see what the CEO has to say about their growth plans for the next three years. It all goes to making you better informed and comfortable in your discussions. It also helps the conversation move forward and it proves you're not just interested in trying to sell them something, but you're genuinely interested in their business.

For example, if you read that they are in a bidding war, winning new deals will mean more work, maybe more staff and more money generated to keep the bottom line healthy. Again, your product or service might be just the thing to help them with the new challenges. It's all about being informed and being prepared.

If you're selling software, they're only concerned about using your product to achieve greater market share in their industry so thoroughly understand it. To set yourself apart from your competition, you might tell them about another company in their sector which has done something similar to them and succeeded.

Meeting rules

If you are invited to sit in a simple meeting room with just chairs and a table, I would always pick the chair furthest from the door if it's not obviously the client's chair.

I do that for four reasons:
1. I am not constantly getting up when new people arrive for the meeting to make room
2. The back of the room is often where the electric plugs are for presentation equipment
3. People usually listen more attentively to speakers sitting in that position in a meeting room, and lastly
4. I have already decided before walking into the meeting that that is where I want to sit, so I don't even think about it and there is no dithering around.

Knowing where I'm going to sit gives me one less thing to worry about before I begin to speak.

Finally, if you are offered a drink, choose water, or get used to drinking black coffee. They are both easy for the client to make.

In summary, I am prepared in advance because my laptop is fully charged and I have VGA and HDMI adaptors ready, and I have a backup on a memory stick if all else fails. From personal preference I have a slide deck (usually 5-6 slides long) which is fairly generic so I could present this to a private or public sector organisation with similar high-impact and conversation-provoking effect. A few days before the meeting, I start to personalise my slide deck with the customer's logo and a couple of points that I've already discussed over the phone about how my product addresses their issues and the value we bring to the table. I have cleared my brain of all distractions just as I made sure my clothes were ready the night before, my shoes were clean, and my hair was neatly cut.

Remember that plans seldom survive contact with the enemy, and so a meeting will almost never go the way you think it will. There will be the odd question you can't answer, and something may go wrong with your technology, so be prepared to pivot in that

moment and recover. However, there are some rules
I use in every meeting:

- Stand until the client sits
- Ask if anyone else is joining us
- Open the meeting with "Thank you for seeing me today, I know you are very busy, so I'll try to ensure your time is not wasted"
- "Before we get into the conversation, can we go around the table and make our introductions?"
- Ensure you start and have a 30 second introduction on who you are and what you do for your company. Be enthusiastic from the outset
- Write down everyone else's name and title as they are talking to show you are listening as they speak. Writing their names in the positions they sit around the table will also help you use people's names later in the meeting when you might have forgotten who's who and also help you with the HUGELY IMPORTANT follow up email later.
- Start the meeting with a question: "Dave, the last time we talked to set up this meeting, you said you were thinking about this type of technology and were scanning the market for options. Is that correct?"

Be concise. Much depends on the type of meeting you are having. At the start, they probably don't know much about you, they're just curious and they may not yet have a compelling event to make a purchase. However, you have got the opportunity to capture their attention and normally, because you've done your research, you know they would benefit from your product. At the very least, by the end of the meeting they know a little bit more about your product and service and they can start to think how they could use it and how it could be useful to them.

Departure
With enterprise or B2B sales, you rarely get the opportunity to walk away with an order at the first

meeting, but you should try to reach a level of agreement that I call "mutual action points."

Before closing the meeting, I always aim to get agreement on the points that were important to the client as well confirm who's doing what. I may have agreed to come back with pricing details, while the customer is going to share the product information with their procurement department and business unit. I also aim for us to agree to have a round-up call or follow-up meeting in three weeks and, in the meantime, I will answer any technical questions we weren't able to cover in the first meeting.

Remember, do not leave the meeting without an agreement on the points that were important to the client, and make sure you have confirmed the next steps. Then close with an agreement about the next contact call or meeting. **All you're doing is a mini close and it's your job as a salesperson to be on top of this process.**

You want to leave the customer realising how passionate you are about your product or service and how knowledgeable you are about their company. A good sign is if they quiz you closely. You want them to be asking you pertinent questions about your business and press you for more information about your product because that shows they are interested. They in turn will be asked tough questions by their own procurement department and they will have to defend their decisions.

Power of the follow-up
I always follow up the appointment with an email to say thank you for the meeting, to restate the action points we agreed and, hopefully, we shared something interesting to think about. I reiterate what I pledged to do and, if a follow up meeting was scheduled, send a calendar invitation. I ask that, if

there was anything I had missed out, please correct me.

Not only is a thank you note good manners, but it also keeps the lines of communication open and leads to further discussions at a specific date. Do not bypass this important step, it will set you apart from your less well-trained competitors I assure you.

A final tip

The first face-to-face meetings can always seem daunting. If you are not with a colleague to talk to, try the **Box Breathing** technique devised by the US Navy Seals. After 26 years I am used to presenting but at the start I used this method to calm my nerves: Imagine a square box. Breathe in for four seconds as you go up one side of the box. Hold your breath for four seconds as you travel across the top. Breathe out for four seconds as you descend the other side. Hold for another four seconds as you move across the bottom of the square. Repeat four to five times and your nerves will settle and your thoughts will clear.

Summary

- **First Impression** - You must be a social chameleon
- **The Greeting** – When in doubt about what to say resort to **F.O.R.M: Family, Occupation, Recreation and Money**
- **Be Prepared** - Before your appointment, research their company and their industry, read their board messages and papers if they are in the public domain and see what the CEO has to say
- **Meeting Rules** – Choose the chair furthest from the door
- **Departure** - Never leave a meeting without agreeing on mutual action points

- **Power of the follow up** – Always follow up with a thank you. It's good manners and it keeps lines of communication open
- **Box Breathing** – first meetings can be daunting, so use Box Breathing to calm the nerves.

Resources

<u>**Box Breathing**</u>

6.Working with Pre-sales

If you think of Pre-sales as just a backroom facility which you can call on as and when it suits your sales agenda, then you are wasting 99% of a valuable resource and you are plain wrong. If the salesperson is the architect of a deal, then pre-sales is the project manager who can demonstrate precisely to the customer what you are trying to sell.

Pre-sales is something of a misnomer - it should be thought of as 'solutions engineering.'

The pre-sales role is to understand:
- the prospective client's issues
- what the customer wants from a technical point of view and from a product point of view
- what the customer wants to get out of the product you are selling

Then, pre-sales can build a presentation, demo or proposal that talks technically to that customer's brief. In short, **the goal of pre-sales in all of this is to secure a technical fit in the prospective client's mind.**

Time for pre-sales
When is it time to call in pre-sales to help push through a deal? The answer is that it's never too soon.

There is a right time and a wrong time to reach for your pre-sales resource. Before even thinking about calling on pre-sales, you will have made at least one and probably more **discovery calls** to glean as much information as possible about the customer's requirements, what their current situation is and how urgently they need to find a solution to their problem. The more information you can get to bring back inside your company, the more chance you have of enticing pre-sales into doing some work with you. You must re-assure them that this is worth their time.

The worst approach you can make to pre-sales is to say, "I have a potential client, I don't really know too much about them, but can pre-sales please do their usual presentation on Monday." If you take that approach, where there has been no good qualification or discovery of the prospect, pre-sales are unlikely to want to help you ever again, because they also want to feel that they are being treated as partners with you in any opportunity, rather than being the "demo department".

Unless they're very, very good, without that basic background to a customer, discussions will stall. Thankfully, I've worked with some first-class pre-salespeople who were able to pivot almost 90 degrees at will and talk about completely different subjects where I either haven't done that qualification thoroughly enough (and yes, we all make mistakes) or the customer just decided to go off on a tangent. Essentially, you need to know what the customer is looking to buy, what quantity and when, before you even think about talking to pre-sales. There are very few of these first-class types of pre-salespeople around. They are in high demand when you have them, so be careful to do your part of the bargain. Even the best pre-salespeople will respect you for doing the necessary research.

What do pre-sales do?
What selling is trying to do is prove the concept, or better still, prove the value of the investment by the customer in the product. To do that requires a partnership: one is the salesperson, account executive or account director, and the other is pre-sales. There is no pecking order; the salesperson runs the deal and will be measured on the deal and its

progression. But the pre-salesperson is an equal partner, and they will be measured on how well they presented the solution. You may be running the deal as the salesperson, but you are not necessarily senior to them in the company.

The role of pre-sales is to demonstrate the technical fit. Pre-sales tackles issues for the customer such as:
- "If this software, (for example) were free, would you own it"?
- "Does this do what you want it to do regardless of cost?"
- "Does this fulfil your functional requirements?"
- "Does this do what you need it to do"?

Great. Stop there, now we're talking about quantity and price. The pre-salesperson demonstrates the technical outcomes if the solution were implemented from today over a year or five-year period.

Pre-salespeople look at the whole picture. Is it just that one thing the customer is trying to fix or is it a multitude of challenges? Does the customer's existing product do what's needed? The best pre-salespeople go one step further and identify problems that the customer didn't even know they had or may have in the future. Above all, the presentation must be crystal clear because today you are generally presenting to a committee rather than just to one person. Even if all committee members must sign off on the deal, some may be in the meeting.

As part of the prospects requirement there will be some element of implementation and deployment of the product, maybe in-house training, the technical discovery conversations will uncover this ideally with the help of a technical sponsor within the account. Pre-sales will put their 'hands on the keyboard' with the customer prior to the sale, make sure the technology delivers on the promises and solves the problem.

Everyone's got a problem
It's a truism, but every business has a problem. The real issue for you is to find it. Identify the pain and someone might pay for it to go away.

If you properly identify and quantify the customer's pain, if you have a sponsor and if you have met the economic buyer, then you can execute a proof of value with a document that the customer signs off.

What pre-sales want to do is help build a business case to support the customer's investment and prove that you can solve their problem. One tried and tested way of doing that is by 'walking in their shoes'. Spending time seeing how the customer operates will quickly demonstrate any flaws in their system, which in turn may lead to additional sales.

Sales is a hyper-competitive industry where the detail counts and where being proactive in finding out what the customer needs counts for everything. Even when they don't know what they need, you can help guide them rather than just be reactive.

Everything has a process
Every deal has a process, which also involves coping with bureaucracy and red tape. But process is more about consistent, disciplined execution of the initial research. This is typically the job of the salesperson.

You have your account list; each client has a problem and a specific objective and requires some solution to solve that problem. The disciplined approach is always for sales to dig deeper before pre-sales get involved. Then there should always be a quick preparatory call with pre-sales, so they understand the issues and are able to create a targeted demonstration. You will be able to deliver faster something that is relevant to the customer if pre-sales are briefed fully about what you have learned about the customer and their issues.

A disciplined approach is like a football team that wins 3-2 and, after celebrating the victory, sits down and analyses where it went wrong and allowed in two goals. You should always be working out what could have been done better (Was there proper discovery? Should pre-sales have been better briefed?) so, you are separating the performance from the result.

Firewalls and Continuity
In an ideal world there would be one pre-salesperson for every salesperson, but this is not an ideal world, and the ratios are seldom so generous. It is common for there to be just one pre-salesperson for four or five salespeople.

Pre-sales want to know whether spending a further three hours on your particular deal is time well spent. This becomes a particular issue when sales teams are competing for pre-sales' time. Firewalls get put up as work schedules are consulted and spreadsheets and are created that make calculations about how many hours should be devoted to a particular sale.

From your point of view as a salesperson, you want continuity. Customers get annoyed if the same issues already covered in earlier conversations arise with a different pre-salesperson.

The way round this is to have dedicated teams of sales and pre-sales people where all the projects are discussed together in detail so everyone is up-to-speed and priorities can be allocated. Such "pod" systems are led by a sales director, but the pre-salespeople report to their own departments - a critical issue because pre-sales have other responsibilities and different needs. Each pod becomes a team effort where calendars are coordinated and, most importantly, the customers don't get frustrated by disjointed presentations.

Things will go wrong
There is no escaping the fact that things do occasionally go wrong when presenting to the customer. Pre-sales rightly pride themselves on doing a good job, but if the laptop freezes or someone accidentally kicks out the plug, it is time to adapt and that is when pre-sales can show their mettle. Sometimes you may face a technical win but a commercial failure because the customer suddenly changes their mind, but a technical failure through a lack of preparation or flexibility is unacceptable.

You may lose the deal if you fail to provide a compelling proof of concept or because another vendor did a better presentation. That probably means you were unable to react to changing circumstances or the customer created demanding last-minute requirements. As discussed earlier, you may have been unable to pivot and adapt. The very best pre-salespeople know their own product so well that they can react on-the-spot and say, "While that element is not part of this presentation, I can explain exactly how our solution would perform in this new situation." A train driver just must follow the tracks, but the captain of a ship may be blown off course. Working as a team, be confident enough to be able to go off-topic and adjust the presentation– sales can fill in while pre-sales switch the demo to answer the question.

Shifting emphasis

Salespeople must recognise, however, that there are changes in emphasis in the way pre-sales are working. Today there is a greater demand for deeper discovery and having more information before engaging pre-sales support.

In times gone by, a cursory call with an expression of interest would have been sufficient to set up a meeting. Today, the time being spent on a client by pre-sales can be accurately tracked and sales have to justify their plan and be able to say, "The customer is definitely interested, they're talking to three other competitors, and they are ready to do a deal."

However, if you as a salesperson qualify well, you're going to get great pre-salespeople working with you to play their part. This results in a well-oiled and disciplined execution of discovery. You will have built the customer sponsor and delivered flawless proof of value covering all the requirements. Plus, you will have demonstrated what more your product can do, based upon capabilities that excite the customer. Then, the deal is yours.

Summary:
- **Pre-sales or solutions engineering** – their goal is to secure a technical fit in the client's mind
- **When to call in pre-sales** - you have made your discovery calls and got some solid information about the client's needs
- **What do pre-sales do** - the best ones identify problems that the customer didn't even know they had or will have in the future
- **Everyone's got a problem** - identify the customer's pain and someone might pay for it to go away.
- **Everything has a process** - process is about consistent, disciplined execution.
- **Firewalls and continuity** – a dedicated team of sales and pre-sales removes firewalls and ensures continuity of presentations.
- **Things will go wrong** – be prepared to adapt to technical and commercial changes.

Resources
The Great Demo book by Peter E. Choan

7.Qualification

Qualification is the core skill of the salesperson in B2B or Enterprise Sales. There are various methodologies you can use, but they all amount to holding a carefully crafted conversation with the buyer. It's a two-way process of getting to know one another – what does the buyer need and what do you have to offer. But at the heart of it all is a secret ingredient upon which every deal depends. But let's save that for later.

Selling is really about questions and answers. It's most noticeable when the right questions haven't been asked of the client and you don't know the answers to the qualification questions. Expect rolling eyes from your Sales Director and a P45 to follow.

To put yourself in the best possible position, you need to know what the right questions are and how to get the prospective customer to give you the most meaningful answers.

Methodologies
First let's look at a variety of methodologies.

There are numerous acronyms for these methodologies, including SCOTSMAN, BANT, MEDDIC, MEDDPIC, MEDICAL (and most people mix and match them). They are all tried and tested so none should be dismissed too quickly. If nothing else, these acronyms provide a common language for sales teams to understand, regardless of which one the basic principles are the same:
• The strength of a client's business case to us and
• The strength of our proposed solution against the client's needs.

All qualification methods amount to a useful checklist for showing you have asked the right questions and have some answers direct from the client. This is helpful for your solution partners too if they are good salespeople.

Applying a methodology is never as simple as asking the customer to provide answers to each element, given that you and your clients are not robots. In the ebb and flow of a conversation, the last thing you want to do is stop, read your cue card and spout "What are your metrics?" The client will look at you like you have arrived on the first bus from Mars and quickly get rid of you for fear that you are in some way having a melt-down.

In order to get the qualification information, you have to use the right words. Here are a few phrases you might like to try. Feel free to change them to fit your own style, and layer them into your sales conversations. I must admit that I'm blunter than most people, so you may want to soften these a little after you test them in your own meetings:

Questions for the customer that lead the conversation for Impact of the issue:

"Is cost, efficiency or some other business need important to you in this situation?"

"What does good look like?"

"How would success be measured by the wider business?"

Questions for the customer that lead the conversation around obtaining the money (budget is not always sitting there waiting for you to claim it, more often these days you need to help the business find the budget):

"Let's say you and I come to an agreement. Is there anybody else, who would need to be involved or approve going ahead?"

"Are you the project sponsor with sign-off for the budget?

"What does success look like to you, others, or the business?"

"What are the next steps if my proposal fulfils your success criteria?"

Questions for the customer that lead the conversation around the decision:

"Who needs to approve the decision?"

"Are there any formal boards or meetings scheduled to discuss this type of decision?"

"How have you done this type of purchase in the past?"

"Do you have a process for purchases such as this?"

"Is there a formal process in your project approval workflow?"

"How long does the decision process usually take?"

Questions for the customer that lead the conversation for decision criteria:

"What are the technical criteria that must be met to make a decision?"

"How do you calculate the Return on Investment (ROI) for this project and what level of ROI is expected?"

"Do you have to complete a business case document, and can I help you with any of that data?"

Questions for the customer around the process of getting the order in terms of the sign off through the business and an order landing in your inbox:

"Who are the people involved and what are the steps to reach the decision?"

"How are these steps put in a sequential order and what is the timeline?"

"Are your procurement team aware of this process and when can we meet them?"

"How does the approval process look for an order to be processed of £100k, £500k or over £1m?"

"How is the legal construct set up?" how will you work together formally?"

"Are there frameworks or particular partners we need to work with?"

"What are your terms and conditions that I need to review or are you happy to review ours?"

"Will your legal team need to oversee this process and if so can we have a meeting soon to discuss?"

Questions for the customer on identification of pain and impact of that pain:
"What causes delays for you?"

"What does a delay mean for you, your team or the wider business?"

"What's the consequence of doing nothing and why do anything now?"

"How does this impact your business?"

Questions for you that relate to your sponsor:
Why is this person a sponsor and have we tested them?

Has this person any influence?

What is his or her personal interest in the success of our bid?

Will he or she stand up for you and sell for you when you are not there?

Questions for you that relate to how you relate to the customer's view of the market and competition:

Our strengths and weaknesses?

Their strengths and weaknesses

Who are their sponsors?

How are they competing against us?

What traps have you set for the competitors to fall into? (Play to your strengths and their weaknesses)

Why will we win?

What "gives and gets" are relevant for this negotiation?

Why us, why now why do anything?

Another great set of questions is around the client's ability or motivations to change, and if they do why will they do something with your company?

"What are the consequences of doing nothing?"

"Is our solution/service/product unique or at least in front of the competition enough to make the client choose us?

What you are trying to do is help the customer by asking those questions, so you both are clear about the problem they are trying to solve, what is holding them back and impacting their revenue, what constitutes a disaster for them and how fast they are able to move to fix it.

I urge you to practise these questions with colleagues and try them out with your clients. Even if you get to ask only two or three questions, you will feel great when your client tells you the answers. And you will have some details to put into your Salesforce system or other Customer Relationship Management system. You can also stand up strongly to questions that may be asked in internal meetings about your sales forecast.

The qualification process in practice

With all methodologies, there needs to be a problem that is quantifiable. For instance, how big is the problem and how do you quantify it?

That's a question that you should ask the customer:
- Is this problem costing you £1,000,000 a year?
- Is this problem stopping you from moving forward in some way?
- Is this problem eating away at your bottom line?
- What is the impact on your bottom line and how much do you think this is costing you now?

There are good reasons for asking these questions:
- If your solution costs £1.5 million and their problem is costing only £1,000,000, then you know they're never going to buy your product.
- If you're talking to a major organisation and their problem costs only £10,000 a year, the chances are that's probably not the biggest problem on their agenda. On the other hand, if you are dealing with a medium-sized business, £10,000 could be a very appropriate problem to deal with.

Therefore, you need to get an idea of how important a problem is to that business – the **pain points** which could include loss of revenue or customer satisfaction (with a backlog of callers in a call centre) or a training issue. The size and nature of the problem suggests the seniority of the people who will likely be making the final decision.

Whatever the problem is, your product must address that and must be a good fit in terms of:
- Yes, we can address that problem, and

- The cost of buying the solution must be less than the problem costs, even over a period of time.

The Decision Makers

These days there are far more people involved in a decision in enterprise deals. Some of them you will know, and you will be in contact with, or you should be in contact with, and some of them you won't know (yet). These are the people that hide in the shadows and don't ever come to the meetings, but they are part of the decision process.

Who is the financial decision maker or budget owner?

There's always a person with the final yes or no, so it's best if you can speak to that budget holder and see if they agree that this is a problem and crucially if they've got the budget to do anything about it. Perhaps, more importantly these days, can they find the budget to do anything about it?

The second step is to ensure that the budget can accommodate your product's cost. Remember also that there are others who will have an influence over the final decision: the people who would use the product; the people who would manage the people that would use the product; and the people who would be involved in implementing the product (perhaps technical staff who would be part of that decision process or decision-making activity). You may not get to meet them all, but you need to be sure that everyone understands that they have this problem, that they are motivated to solve it, and they are leaning towards your solution.

The process to get a Purchase Order raised

This is the process for making decisions in an organisation.

If, for example, you are dealing with a customer who has traditionally bought your kind of software technology before, you need to ask if they can explain the purchasing process they use. The chances are that if they had the software, they wouldn't have the problem. Or they may be like a government organisation which will have a purchasing and tendering process.

So, you've established that there might be different levels of sign-off to go through:
• Technical fit - the initial decision that shows your solution tackles their problem
• Conviction - the knowledge that other customers of yours are using the product successfully and
• Budget - there is enough money in the kitty.
These three levels are the cohort of decision makers; everyone is involved in the paper chain; they've had a demonstration, or they've gone through proof of concept.

To secure payment from the organisation, you must go back to that finance director to get agreement. And, finally, there may be a separate buyer who makes the purchase.

Without asking the basic qualifying questions in that buying process, you will struggle to land the deal. It all speaks to why they want your product and the volume they are going to buy. It is also important to know roughly when they are going to buy, because that comes back into the forecasting: when do I see this deal concluding? Is it this month? Is it this quarter? Is it next quarter? Is it next year? You need to understand when that decision will be taken and when that paperwork process is likely to come to an end.

A word about Sponsors.

You are not alone in this sales process. Sometimes there will be people in the target company that are helping you. These are your sponsors who will be your advocates inside the customer's decision-making team. They may have introduced you in the first place, but they are there so you can take the temperature of the sale on a regular basis. Sponsors can help you find out how the process is going, whether the company is considering a rival and, perhaps, where you stand in the ranking of potential suppliers.

Always beware

The more questions you ask the better. However, be warned: **the customers may not always tell you the truth**. This may be because they do not know the whole truth (which is not necessarily their fault) but may not want to seem like they don't know the whole truth. So, they might make up a bit of their story just to look like they know what they're talking about and appear in control. Or they may give you an answer anyway, just to keep you happy, so take care that you are not seen to be "leading the witness."

You must always verify the answers you obtain. You can do this by double checking with others in the customer's team, including your sponsor. When a commitment to buy a product is made and a date is given, establish why. It is very easy for deadlines to slip, and this happens because you did not verify answers you obtained in the qualification process. And you don't just ask your questions once - ask them through all stages of the selling process: are we still on for the end of the month? Are you confident you have still got the budget? The more senior the management level you deal with, hopefully, the more accurate the answers you get.

Never be worried about asking too many questions. In business-to-business selling, the buyer expects to be quizzed. Always ask permission first by saying something like, "It's great that you're on this call and fantastic that you're looking at our product. First, may I ask what's the problem you're trying to solve?" And then "I would really like to ask a lot more questions. Is that OK with you?" The answer is obviously going to be "yes", or why else would they be on the call? My favourite question is "What's the latest you can make this purchase to align with your time scales?" Because it enables the prospective client to think about their own deadlines and work backwards to a purchase date.

Alarm bells

Be alert for the warning signals. One thing that should always rings alarm bells is if key people stop turning up for meetings. If they stop coming (or even if they stop participating in the meetings), you've got a problem.

That's less about asking questions and more about just watching them and watching the process to be able to spot these tell-tale signs. You've asked all the right questions, and you've been polite about it without sounding too much like an interrogator, but you notice absences, or timelines are allowed to slip. Much of it comes down to your gut feel while gently but regularly testing and probing as much as you can.

The secret ingredient

Now here is that vital secret ingredient promised at the start of this chapter. The secret ingredient is EMOTION.

You must be aware that the key factor in qualification is that all decisions are made emotionally, even in business.

First comes the emotion and then follows the justification with facts. Just think about why you bought your latest gadget – a phone, a laptop, and iPad or even a car. What appealed to you first? Was it the superior connection? The technology or the reliability? Or was it really the look, the feel, the comfort, the speed? You made your mind up first on an emotional level and then you set about thinking of all the technical benefits to JUSTIFY your emotional decision. At least, that's what happens if you're like 99% of all other people.

The same thing applies in enterprise sales. Your product may be superior, but, if you are too pushy and aggressive in your questioning, the buyer will not want to deal with you and will then set about justifying their decision by looking for real or imagined flaws in your presentation. It is impossible to take the emotion out of the purchasing process. That is why you must come across first as seeking to understand the customer's problem. When it comes down to the final decision, there may be no difference between your product or your competitors'. The winner will be based on likeability not technology because, quite simply, we are all emotional beings.

High level bullets, for a happy leader

In most situations your sales leaders will want to know a few things to give them comfort around a particular deal, it comes down to these questions. If you can answer these questions off the top of your head without checking the CRM system, you will look in control of the deal and have a plan. I urge you to commit this to memory and, on important and/or large deals, have this information quickly to-hand:

- What is the size of the deal to your organisation?
- When will this deal hit the books and close?
- Why will the client buy from us over the competition?
- What's the motivation to change the status quo?
- What's the steps to close, or at least the next three steps and have you agreed these with the client?
- Any risks you foresee?

Clearly, in a deal-review meeting situation, you will need to have this to hand and the deeper detail behind it, but you will have time to prepare, and others involved in the deal attending the same meeting. Essentially, the key questions come back to:

"How much?" "When?" "What's the risk?" and "What do we do next?"

Summary:

- **The right questions** – the best questions are the ones that get the best answers. Without them there is no deal
- **Decision makers** – identify and focus on the key decision makers who may be in the background
- **Process** – understand the purchasing process of the client
- **Sponsors** – identify and use your sponsor to monitor the selling process
- **Red Flags** – watch for the warning signals of absences and slipping deadlines
- **Emotion** - all buying decisions are made emotionally
- **Have the basics in your head**- your leadership need to know you understand the deal inside and out and you know what to do next.

Resources that you might find useful:
Bant – www.salesodyssey.com
Scotsman – www.advancescotsman.com
MEDDIC – www.meddic.academy
Force Management -
https://www.forcemanagement.com

8.Leadership

Remember what you learnt in chapter three – you are the CEO of your own operation. So, whether you are boss of a company or boss of your patch, the same leadership skills apply. In fact, you should be harder on yourself if you let yourself down by your own performance.

Equipped with some of the tools you have already picked up, you are more than ready to perform. But first consider the following character traits that you might need to polish!

In this chapter I'll use the terms "leader" and "Manager" interchangeably however my view of a leader is someone who motivates a team, ensures they are accountable and looks further into the future and brings the team along with them in building that future collaboratively if at all possible, whereas a Manager should be a leader but often is simply keeping the train on the rails that have been already built it's up to you to decide which type you are going to be and which type you work for.

Attitude
When a manager is putting a sales team together, they want to be sure of certain instinctive behavioural qualities. The primary quality is **attitude**.

Think about a football team of exceptionally talented individuals who have a brilliant track record for scoring goals. But if for some reason one of the players has the wrong attitude, this person is like a rotten apple in a barrel and will soon affect the rest of the squad, no matter how good the other players are. Irrespective of how talented a salesperson is, no matter how often they hit their target, sooner or later their poor attitude will create a poor atmosphere and disrupt the culture of the whole team.

As a salesperson, put yourself in the position of your manager and ask yourself if you are performing to the best of your ability AND performing as a team player. What is your attitude like? Are you constantly coming up with problems or are you proposing solutions, perhaps to finding new leads? No-one wants a manager who is constantly criticising, so how are you tackling your own problems as your own CEO?

You have probably been given an area to cover which might be just a post code or an entire region, so what is your plan? If you are struggling, ask for advice because if you don't ask, you are not making that extra effort. You have the wrong attitude.

What managers want to see is that you're trying. They want to know that when you have a rejection, when you have your nose bloodied and the door slammed in your face more than once, that you have that mental resilience to pick yourself up, ask where you went wrong, change your approach and try again. No-one expects good-news stories all the time, so you shouldn't expect them of yourself. Critique your plan and find a new approach.

Your DNA
As part and parcel of attitude, any manager wants to know what drives you as an individual - what's in your DNA. Are you modest or arrogant, what motivates you, is it money, the job, your commission at the end of the month? There is nothing wrong with that, but it paints a picture and shows if you are a team player and likely to stay in the company for any length of time as if there is a significant amount of work to be done before the area is delivering business

and commission then there are types that will be suited to this area and others that will no. Equally there is nothing wrong with being driven, but it is a character trait which needs to be managed.

A manager wants to know that you can be trusted to pursue a $1,000,000 deal and represent your company well. The customers also want to understand your mindset. Can you and your company be trusted to support them: do you genuinely care about the customer getting the best value out of the investment or are you just interested in doing a hit-and-run sale and then walking away, leaving the customer with no backup?

As a salesperson sitting in front of the customer presenting your product, you need to display an attitude that creates a connexion, builds the right chemistry, and radiates the integrity that comes with representing a responsible company that sells high value products. The customer needs to believe in you and to trust you, because, as far as they are concerned, you are 'the company'. When you sit in front of the customer, not only are you asking them to part with real money, but also you are asking them to put their careers on the line to some extent because, when they spend a $1,000,000 of their company's money, they're going to be held accountable if it turns out to be a poor decision.

Transparency
Trust between you and your customer client must exist between you and your manager. It is a two-way street. When
you tell your manager that the deal is going to happen, your sales manager must trust you because they will be reporting that information up the chain of command and it must be correct. If it turns out not to be true, it becomes your manager's problem as well as yours. Then, the next time you say you're

making progress and are about to close, you won't be believed and, if a round of head-count reductions is announced, your name will likely be on the list.

Be up front and clear with your manager, say when you are facing obstacles, and remember to ask for help. Various Customer Relations Management (CRM) systems are widely used to track progress, so a sales manager can always see what the team is doing and how sales are progressing. But these CRM systems are only as good as the information that is posted into them.

Say what you do and do what you say

This is an old saying but wise, nonetheless. Just as you need to be transparent in your CRM postings, you need to deliver on your promises.

Talk about what you're doing, talk about where you are with your leads, what the potential risks are and what the potential upside might be. Explain how the deal is going to be shaped. Is it going to start as a small deal and then become a bigger contract later?

Explaining how often you are getting to see the customers shows your transparency, by actually doing what you are saying is integrity.

Your own leader must also be open with the sales team. If things are not going well, the leader needs to say so early in order to turn the situation around, and if things are progressing well, the team can celebrate and call out the talent so people can follow the pattern of that success, is a team effort, and no rotten apples.

Staying power

Whether you are building a sales team or just joining a new company, the corporate atmosphere is important. Selling is not a solo activity - you must get out and drive your own sales' cycle, but you are also part of a group, part of the company, part of a team. As a leader, you have to make sure that your employer continues to come across to your team as a great place to work. I it is not a great place to work, you will start losing your team as soon as they get an offer from another company that is a better place to work, where the pay is good, the product is easy to sell, and they'll get no hassle from administration.

|It takes about three years to get a new recruit up-to-speed. As a rookie salesperson, you may only achieve a small sales quota in your first year. You've got to learn the ropes and develop your accounts. In the second year, your sales will grow, and your third year is when the company really begins to see a return on the investment that they have made in you. When you are hired, the company is looking for people who they can predict will be successful, and who are going to stay for at least three years. After that, you will either decide to climb the corporate ladder internally or you will leave or be headhunted. When you become a manager yourself, you will, in turn, be judged on your ability to hire the right team and be able to motivate them and keep them together for at least three years in order to build a continuity of the relationship with customers.

Dealers in Hope

If a manager runs day-to-day operations, then, as Napoleon Bonaparte said: "*A leader is a dealer in hope.*"

You may have a leader who comes to sales meetings and just puts their head in their hands saying, "I don't know where this is going to go guys, I really haven't got a clue where the next deal is coming from." If you hear that, you probably know it's time to move on. The best leaders are the ones who have done the hard graft, they've been in the trenches, and they have faced the bullets themselves to use some military metaphors. You will follow them, and they will follow you because they believe in what you are selling. Also, they know there will be rejections, but they will encourage you to overcome setbacks, and they will keep you informed about great new products on the horizon that will need working groups of multi-skilled people including a salesperson too. Such leadership generates optimism and encouragement because you have faith in your leader that they are taking a six-to-twelve-month view. Sharing that view with you shows there is a future and that's what keeps you interested. **They are dealing in hope.**

When you join a team, the leader should say, "I've got your back, I will set you up for success." This is a great example of giving before asking for something in return. With the right tools and the right training, any salesperson can generate a pipeline and succeed. A leader is not doing the sales job for you, never micro-managing, but must always be ready to help where they can. And be strong enough to admit when they too have made a mistake They need to be on your side and help remove internal corporate barriers as you push your ideas further up the chain of command, because they trust you, because you do what you say you will do, they will support you.

The simplest definition of leadership is, 'to get things done through and with people'. That means, as a leader you, must inspire, coach, reward and motivate every member of the team in every department. Then, you are enabling people to perform. A good leader is not always holding their people immediately accountable - people need the space and freedom to manoeuvre and even, at times, make mistakes.

79

There is a huge difference between a manager and a leader:

• A manager is someone who runs a machine. They keep on doing the same thing repeatedly, making sure the train doesn't run off the rails and the team cranks out some results. A manager looks to maintain the status quo in most cases.

• A leader can maintain the status quo, but also diversify. They know that they need to have multiple things in play - some will work, and some may fail. A leader must identify where the team ought to go and deals with aspirations and future challenges, while a manager handles the here and now, and deals with today's problems.

From a sales perspective when a manager says they want to offer you help with a deal, it's got to be the right kind of help. Some help is just an opportunity to inspect the deal, and that's not really going to help anyone. If the help is to advise, encourage or suggest a different approach, then that is the kind of help to welcome.

Remember that you are a salesperson in charge of your own franchise. You must inspire those above:

• Inspire your manager to support you when you go to your marketing department and ask them to put on a promotional event for you, or

• Inspire a senior colleague to support you at your next client meeting when you are certain that, with their backing, you can push the deal over the line.

By being able to communicate bold ideas, at the management level or the sales level, is what good looks like in a business. 'Good' is not only being able to fill your pipeline with quality leads and being able to hit your target numbers, but also being able to have a strong rapport with your boss, so you can admit when things are going wrong and seek advice. A recruit doesn't join a company or for the money (in most cases); they join a leader who has inspired them with confidence and who will set them up for success. In much the same way, your senior colleagues will gladly come to your client meetings because they believe in you. No organisation is going to achieve its numbers if the culture the atmosphere, the moods and the skills are not in harmony.

Bad doesn't just happen

Of course, life is not always harmonious, and things do go wrong. But 'bad' does not just happen.

You don't just walk into the office one day and 'bad' happens to you. If you are not getting enough leads, then put your hand up early and say so. It is a shared responsibility between you and the business development teams. Don't' sit in silence day after day waiting for an opportunity to be handed to you because, sooner or later, your manager is going to say, "you are not hitting your target, the decision has been taken and we're going to let you go." It may not be your fault, perhaps you were not being managed well, but it was a problem that was building over time, and it was your fault for not raising it sooner.

It comes back to team spirit and behaviour. In the most successful companies' sales are generated by people who **hunt in packs.** That is to say there is a strong bond between all departments, and they all have the same goal in mind, involving sales, marketing, business development, product development and senior management. In this environment, you are never criticised if a deal is lost when you had asked for support from a senior manager to attend a meeting. But expect everyone's criticism if you had failed to use all the resources that were available to you. Equally, you must be ready to offer help when asked. If you're doing the right thing for you, then that should also be the right thing for the team and for the company.

When the revenue is not coming in, what should you do to make a good impression? As a manager and a leader, you have to understand the personalities of the people working for you and with you, because, when you can do that, you also know how to motivate them and how to guide them or hold them accountable without insulting them. And that is always a delicate balance. To make a good impression as a sales representative who doesn't have the revenue, show that you know the steps you have to take to achieve success. Discuss your plan of action with others, take advice and do what you say you are going to do! Above all, show energy and activity because, without energy and activity, nothing happens.

Summary:

Attitude – No matter how talented the team, rotten apples will taint the corporate culture.
Your DNA - Any manager wants to know what drives you as an individual, what's in your DNA.
Transparency - The trust between you and the customer, also must exist between you and your manager.
Say what you do and do what you say - Talk about what you're doing, talk about where you are with your leads, what the potential risks are and what the potential upside might be. Follow up on your words with action.
Staying power – Hire the right team and motivate them to stay.
Dealers in Hope – Leaders are dealers in hope – you will follow them, and they will trust you.

Bad doesn't just happen - You don't just walk into the office one day and bad happens to you – there is always a reason.

Resources:

The Leaders Bookshelf book, by Admiral James Stavridis & Manning Ancell

9. What's in it for me?

WIIFM - What's in it for me?

That is what is in the back of everyone's mind when an offer is on the table. You want to sell a product and the customer is asking themselves, "Why should I buy? What is the benefit to my business?" Or even, "What is the risk?"

Whatever is on offer, most if not all clients will ask you for a discount. You know what they want when they ask: "Can you sharpen your pencil a bit?" or some other euphemism. The question then is how you will react. There will always be room for negotiation, everyone knows that, but have you got your strategy lined up? How much are you ready to give away and when should you make your counteroffer?

Reciprocity

Reciprocity, often referred to as "Give to Get", is at the root of all deals. Give to get is very important and very straight forward, but it is not easy to get it right. It can be dressed up in any number of ways, but everyone wants to believe they have emerged from the negotiations as a winner, which is particularly important if you want to develop a deeper relationship or continue a long-term relationship.

The trouble is, in the heat of the moment, you may not be able to think of some suggestions to offer the client in exchange for the discount, particularly if the request takes you by surprise.

The request for a discount can come at any time during the deal making process. Sometimes, it will be mid-way through the discussion. Sometimes, a request will be made by a business user or technician before submitting your proposal to procurement. At other times, you'll hear directly from the procurement people themselves.

Then what do you do? It can be a wise move to hold your ground. It's certainly not wise to jump in immediately with a discount. It makes you sound cheap or an easy push-over or suggests your price was always too high. If you give way so soon, the customer will go on taking, assuming you will go on giving. However, it's also worth considering accepting the clients' request for a discount, but always ask for something in return. That's "Give-to-get."

But what do you ask for? You may be lost for the words. Remember, you are in business and discounts are there to be traded. Trading is all about giving something of low value to you but high value to the customer, and, in return, their giving something of low value to them but high value to you.

Finding the words

Like the boy scouts, you should "be prepared," always in a state of readiness in mind and body. Be prepared with what you are willing to offer but don't be too free with your discounts. It's very easy to give them away, but you cannot get them back once offered. They are there to be negotiated carefully.

Here are some examples you may want to keep close to hand when that call comes in requesting the dreaded "D-word".

Things to ask for – Initially when speaking with the client this will also help you to help them.

• Executive level access (perhaps for technical information or for lobbying)
• Identified executive sponsor (technical and lobbying)
• Agreement to next steps (in the form of a mutual activity plan)
• Visibility of a strategic plan, a roadmap of action and access to participation

Things to ask for – When you have done most of
the selling

• Time with key people (directors, architects,
developers)
• Agreement on decision criteria and metrics for a
Proof of Concept and the prerequisites for a Proof
of Concept (such as environment, data and
resources)
• Visibility of the data and metrics for the business
case
• Commitment to a timeline for contractual
execution
• Doing the deal on your company's paperwork and
terms
• A request that the Economic Buyer comes to the
Proof of Concept kick off

Things to ask for – in Negotiation stage with the
business

• Term length of three to five years
• A commitment to growth in volume over time
• Become a Beta Customer
• Provide references (case studies, video, executive
calls, analyst calls)
• Competitive product replacement roadmap
• Continued and increasing access to executives
• Participation in company events
• Auto-renewal

The words you use are important when couching
your "give-to-get" and you need to hear the specific
discount from the client in terms of a percentage or
an amount of money. If you simply go to your boss
and say the customer is asking for a discount and you

haven't explored some of these questions, you will be forced to go back and get some answers. Far better to say that you're prepared to take the request for a discount to your sales manager, but you need to know how much is being asked for and what is being offered in return. Internally, it makes you, as a salesperson, look more plausible with your leadership team, and it makes you, as a salesperson. more confident and capable

You could try saying, "I really want to give you what you asked for in terms of the discount. However, I'll need to write a short business case to justify the reduction in price and get my business to make a decision. Can you help me with one of the items in this list (*read from the Early, Mid and Late stage lists above*) as they may be of low value, time, or energy to you, but represent high value to us, and may swing the business' decision to allow me to discount this for you."

I know that's a mouthful and please don't try to memorise it. What you actually say will need to be in your own words.

An example of how this might work in practice could be: "I can request a 10% discount from my business if you are comfortable to be a reference. If you're happy for our marketing people to talk to you about a public reference, that will make my request much easier. You'll obviously get final sign off on anything published and I expect it will have to be approved by your communications department."

Crucially, any arrangement must be contingent on the reference being part of the final contract.

Blockers

You can find yourself going through the sales process and everybody's happy when suddenly the deal lands with somebody in procurement who is charged with getting the best deal. They're only interested in the product and whether it will do what is required. They may even say they can get the same product somewhere else for X amount cheaper than you've been quoting.

To avoid this obstacle, try and talk early on to their procurement person in a mature way to ensure that they have the ability to think of the bigger picture or see if they can put you in front of a more senior executive. (*See Initial, Mid-point and Late stage lists above*).

On the other hand, you may face a curveball at any point in the discussion. Procurement may demand a discount at the very start of negotiations in which case politely decline saying, "I don't know when you want to buy this product and I don't know what your organisation looks like in terms of future potential." So, don't offer anything at that point. They may say, "Well, we've got a genuine requirement, we need this many, and we need to do it this year, but we're on a tight budget, so can you do anything on the price?" If so, you can have a mature and sensible conversation.

Without Prejudice

What you are seeking to achieve in your discussions is what amounts to a pre-contract agreement without prejudice. If you are asked if you can do better on the price being quoted, you can hold an off-the-record conversation. you might suggest that you can ask your business for 10% off, but explain it is not your decision. Suggest that you will need to check with the business. You can add that you are confident you can get you a discount but not without some sort of concession on the customer's part. Then you can leave your suggestions for the customer to think about.

The customer might even say, "Actually, I gave a reference for another organisation a couple of months ago, so I think I can do that for you." At that point, you almost have a pre-contract with the purchasing department. It is a trade of something of low value to them but high value to you.

Note: this is not intended to be any kind of side-letter to the deal or dodgy-dealing, as the discount and the reference should all be noted in the formal quotation (and eventual contract), so both parties know what the deal consists of before signing takes place. The off the record conversation simply removes temporarily the buyer-seller hats and removes some emotional pressure from both sides so together you can try to resolve the issue.

Be comfortable with being a middleman (and not the director empowered to take the final decision) because it enables you to ask the customer to help you build the case internally for offering them such a generous discount. You can explain up-front that, in order to get such a deep discount, there might be several layers of management to get to which takes a particular amount of time, which you think you can do if, for example, the customer can offer a good reference or be able to close quickly.

If you are able to say to your internal team that the customer will buy the product and maybe commit to a long-term relationship (which would be written into the contract), then everyone is happy. In this way, your sales manager knows how much of the product the customer wants, how much they are prepared to pay and when they want it. These three elements are the most important part of any internal communication to your manager.

Observed behaviour
You can view these exchanges as micro-deals that lead to a signed contract all tracked and recorded by exchanges of emails:
• The customer has agreed they have a need for your product – box ticked.
• There is an urgent requirement for your product – box ticked.
• Procurement is going to allow access to their senior management – box ticked.
• They are keen to participate in your training programme on the product – box ticked.

All these steps are observed behaviour. They give you an insight into the customer's thinking and their willingness to do a deal. You're not just asking questions you're observing their behaviour. If they are interested in free training on your product, then they have made the mental step to installing your product in their organisation. Otherwise, why would they be discussing how the training programme works? If they keep taking your calls and keep attending your meetings, then they are interested.

By contrast, if the discussions are more adversarial, then it's best to understand that and take a decision with your manager to stick it out because the deal or the client is significant or move on to other potential customers you have in your pipeline.

Return on Investment

There are times when you can't reduce the ticket price of (say) £10,000. That is when you can make the deal more attractive, perhaps by offering better

value for money by offering all the incentives you have up your sleeve, such as:
• free training
• free tickets to a prestigious customer-based event that you are organising, or
• free upgrades, so the value in the product is seen over many months and years.
The bigger the deal, the more pieces you can have on the board to play with so, effectively, the price goes down and the value goes up to the client.

Equally, there will be occasions when an existing customer wants the same product at a cheaper price for no other reason than they want a discount. There may even be a veiled threat about moving away from your business. If you have nothing else to offer them in terms of benefits or concessions, you must evaluate whether or not you want to retain their custom. This is where reciprocity expires - they just want what you are offering but cheaper, for no apparent reason. You simply have to weigh up whether or not the client is so prestigious and valuable that you cannot let them go.

Summary
• **Give to Get -** reciprocity is at the root of all deals.
• **Finding the Words -** be prepared with what you are willing to offer but don't be too free with your discounts.
• **Blockers -** talk to procurement in a mature way early on to ensure that they have the ability to think of the bigger picture.
• **Without Prejudice -** you are seeking to achieve in your discussions what amounts to a pre-contract agreement without prejudice.
• **Observed behaviour -** gives you an insight into the customer's thinking and their willingness to do a deal.

- **Return on investment** - there are times when you can't reduce the ticket price, so you must decide how valuable the customer really is

Resources
www.saleshacker.com
www.forcemanagement.com
www.kahvay.com

10. Negotiation

Selling and negotiating are not the same. They require distinct behaviours as a salesperson you must be a master of both, read on…

Remember - sales come first and negotiations follow.

My favourite question to a potential customer is: If this product were free and does the job required, would you own it? If the answer to that is yes, then the "sale" is complete. Now it is just a question of price, quantity, and urgency, which is all about "negotiation".

Don't let yourself be drawn in by the perceived status of winning a competition between you and the customer. Negotiation is not a competitive sport. Thinking that negotiation is a competition will not lead to repeat customers nor long-term relationships.

R.A.D. (Kahvay.com)

There are various helpful acronyms used selling. 'R.A.D.' stands for **Relationship, Awareness** and **Demand**, which are the building blocks of selling. Before anything happens, you must build a relationship with the customer, establish their awareness about your product and finally confirm if there is demand. If there is no Relationship, Awareness or Demand, don't even start negotiating.

There's **a great difference between selling and negotiating.** The salesperson creates the relationship, creates the awareness, and creates the demand, and it's then the negotiator who negotiates that deal. It is the negotiator's job to choose the right process and behaviour for the negotiation that is about to happen. Often, the seller and the negotiator are the same person, but one who adopts different mindsets.

If Relationship, Awareness and Demand are all present, you should change your selling behaviour into negotiation behaviour.

You have got to know who you're talking to. If you're dealing with a market trader, then you know you're dealing on price only. However, if you're dealing with somebody who genuinely has the experience, the maturity, and the authority to consider value rather than just price, then you can start to be a bit more creative. For instance, you might ask, "Instead of buying just one product now at $100,000, what if you bought six over six years and we hold the price over that period?" Or "If we agree a deal, can you give me a reference or recommendation?"

There are many different pieces that go into a negotiation to arrive at a point where both you and the customer are happy with the deal. Have three positions before even starting the first conversation:

- The fantastic position of selling your product without giving anything away and at the top price
- The worst position in which you will walk away if the client doesn't agree
- A middle position, which is sometimes called the Zone of Agreement. The Zone of Agreement is where the real negotiation takes place, involving the give and the take (the reciprocity explored in the previous chapter).

Negotiating is Questioning, Listening, Observing, Considering, and responding

If you continue to sell in a negotiation, you'll end up talking too much, giving information away and not being aware of what your counterpart is doing or saying. You'll explain too much, justify your position and, worse, even argue why your position is right and theirs is wrong. The sales persona must mentally disengage when the negotiator takes over.

The highest-level principles of negotiating involve acting in good faith and truthfulness, being genuinely interested in your client getting what they want alongside getting what you want, and building trust, empathy and eventually influence.

P.L.A.N.T. (Kahvay.com)

The different types of negotiation require different processes and behaviours. There is not one way or one style, and usually people rely on a style that makes them feel most comfortable, but which may be sub-optimal for a particular deal.

Instead, choose the appropriate style depending on differing circumstances. The acronym 'PLANT' can be your guide and stands for:

- **Power**
- **Longevity**
- **Advanced**
- **Need**
- **Trust**

Determining the status of PLANT in a negotiation will determine the style of negotiation, which in turn will determine the most appropriate process and behaviours.

- *Power* - whoever has the power has options, and that person will be able to choose how they want to negotiate the deal. The best advice is to open with your most extreme position. You can demand $1,000,000 at the start, always knowing that you would accept $500,000. But, because you put your price on the table first, you take control psychologically.

- *Longevity* - a very important element is to understand how long term you want that deal to last, and how long term you have you been in a relationship. Always think about what's going to happen in the future rather than what has happened in the past.

- *Advanced* - how advanced are you and your skills? The less advanced you are, the more likely you are to use fewer variables and less complexity to keep negotiations simple. Equally, the same will apply to the person you are negotiating with.

- *Need* - do you need them, or do they need you, and do they understand why. Decide whether you need to negotiate with this person in the future, and do you need this person to implement the deal?

- *Trust* - this is the biggest factor in negotiation: do you trust them? If they say 'no', do they mean 'no' or is there room to manoeuvre? When they commit to a deal, will they stick to it? Trust is not built on nice words but on actions and respect. If you can't say 'No,' you will end up saying 'Yes' and you will have to explain to your sales manager why you are not achieving your numbers.

Negotiation behaviours

You can come across as cold, hard, tough, arrogant, dismissive, warm, open, cooperative, pleasant, or collaborative in your negotiations, and sometimes you need to switch between them.

Start with a dialogue of collaboration, but collaboration cannot be done in a mutual way if one of the parties says "No". You must eradicate from your vocabulary 'No,' 'Can't,' 'Won't,' 'Shan't' and focus on the possible.

The Kah-Vay Compass of behaviour shows the key variables.

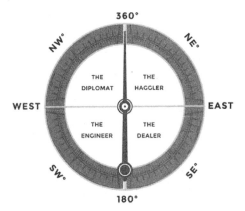

Instinctively each one of us belongs at one point on the compass:
• To the East, we come across as hard and tough, like the haggler or the dealer who says, "This is the price, these are the terms, and there is no room for manoeuvre."
To the West we are warm and cooperative, more like the diplomat or the engineer who says, "Let's see where we can move a little, build a longer (longevity) relationship. Instead of talking about price and volume, let's talk about rebates and contract length"

Not only do you need to understand yourself, but also you need to understand who you're negotiating with. Judge how flexible they might be and adapt to the circumstances. Adapting may well involve moving yourself from one part of the compass of behaviour to another. The compass enables you to analyse your strategy and your tactics, suiting both to the circumstances and the character of your counterpart.

If you are too stubborn or too accommodating, you may leave value on the table. As Daniel Varè, the Italian diplomat and writer, said, *"Diplomacy is the art of letting someone else have your way."* What a lovely way of putting across the right idea of negotiation, too.

The Backdoor
When faced with an outright refusal to budge on price or terms, you can use what I call 'the Backdoor method' which gives your counterparty room for manoeuvre.

Just say, "Look, there are plenty of other things we could do to get you to that price. Do you think we can talk about referrals or length of contract?" Give them time to go away and think about it and more often than not you will have sparked their curiosity.

Follow up with emails if you don't hear back, never, of course, blaming them, but suggesting perhaps they have been very busy with other more pressing priorities. They may apologise for not getting back to you, and it puts the prospective client very slightly on the backfoot.

Name the emotion

If, when you are in the conversation, you see or hear an emotion from the client, you should name the emotion. Say something like "You seem interested in this?" and then silence to allow the client to fill the gap and explain their thoughts. If you see or hear a negative emotion, you should name that too: "You sound like you are not interested in this proposal?" or "It sounds like something is bothering you about this."

They will tell you exactly what's bothering them so you can address it there and then. If you name a positive emotion (such as "You seem really interested in what we have discussed?") that not only adds fuel to that emotion but also strengthens the feeling in the client's mind.

"Naming the Emotion" is also a very powerful tool in controlling your own emotions when in negotiation. While negotiation isn't a competition, it is conflict: one or more parties are coming from different positions to reach an understanding or an agreement. In conflict, our emotions and natural instincts take over. In high conflict situations, many people revert to 'protect and survive' mode and are more inclined to act illogically or irrationally. Tell yourself the emotion you are feeling, and you can help to minimise its impact on your thinking and your behaviour.

Tone and quality of your voice

In essence, there are only a handful of ways to speak. As a salesperson, you need to be aware of them all and which ones to use in different situations to enable you to guide the conversation and gain more information:

- Inflection (i.e., changing the tone up or down) at the end of a statement or a question can change the whole meaning of the words. In a heartbeat, it can make you sound more genuine, or disinterested.
- Inflection used incorrectly will cause alarm bells to ring in the client's mind and they will want to drill into you with more questions, typically about price.

- If your tone is raised at the end of a statement, what you've said becomes a question or an upbeat suggestion. This, followed by a pause, is a great way to elicit more information from a client as they fill the gap in the conversation with more information.

- If your tone is lowered at the end of a statement, what you've said sounds sad or downbeat.
- If you keep your voice flat, then your statement becomes an insistent demand.

Use the same words but with a different tone creates a different meaning:
My Price is...
£1,000,000 (raised tone at the end - implying a question that invites a challenge)
£1,000,000 (consistent flat tone - implying a statement that shows confidence)
£1,000,000 (lowered tone at the end - implying doubt that invites negotiation)

The quality of your voice is especially important if you are on the phone or recording a video. You do not want to sound robotic or like you are reading from a card.

If sounding robotic is one end of a scale, then a soft, graceful, low tone of voice is at the other. It is comforting and measured, warm and inviting regardless of the heated responses you may be receiving. If you are in rapport with someone, it's difficult for them to keep ranting and raving if you stay cool and calm with a warm voice.

Setting the agenda
It is important to set the agenda early on, so that by the time you get to the meeting, both sides know what is to be discussed and there is no conflict in the conversation. In addition, an early question demonstrates real interest in achieving mutual success: "This is what interests us and we think this is of interest to you. Are there other points you would like to address?"

Don't even put a price on the product so that, when it comes to the conversation, you've already given them a bit of time to prepare for what they could do in those other deal variables. And, by avoiding price, you've also indicated that you're willing to be creative, you're willing to be collaborative and you are giving some information. Never give away all the information all in one go. Just release information bit-by-bit to test the water, inviting them to reciprocate: "I've given you something to help you, will you give me something to help me?"

Failing to set an agenda up-front can lead to a conflict orientation where you can freeze and react by saying, "Well, if you can't pay that price, we could consider this (lower) price?" Value is immediately lost.

Setting the agenda is all about discovering what is important for the client and allowing them to discover what's important for you. This is where you get that chance to frame your meetings and start to suggest what could be within an acceptable framework.

The agenda is a beautiful tool when used properly. It is not long-winded but uses snappy bullet points: "We want to talk about X, Y & Z and we think you want to talk about A, B &C. Is this true and can you add to this list?" For the first time you might find out something that you never knew that they were interested in and all because you were open with your information. You have shown trust by sharing what matters to you.

Finally, follow up a meeting with a summary.

Closing is all about summary, summary, summary. Success is about keeping a record of offers all the way through your discussions, summarising frequently to avoid any misunderstanding ahead of the next stage of negotiations. This might mean helping your counterparty negotiate with their own internal stakeholders when you are not in the room, which could be done in a brief two-page summary document that they could sign-off. This demonstrates that you are continuing to collaborate with them, knowing that they are now the negotiators (internally) of the deal.

Remember, you may think you have done a good deal, but it might have been a much better deal with forward planning, because you didn't find out with an outline agenda what the other party could have done up-front.

Summary

- **R.A.D.** - If there is no Relationship, Awareness or Demand, don't even start negotiating.
- **Negotiating is: Questioning, Listening, Observing, Considering** - if you continue to sell in a negotiation, you may give away too much and not be aware of what your counterparty is saying.
- **P.L.A.N.T.** (Power, Longevity, Advanced, Need, Trust) - the status of PLANT in a negotiation will determine the style of negotiation which in turn will decide the most appropriate process and behaviours.
- **Negotiation behaviours** - wherever you are on the compass of behaviour, be ready to move.
- **The Backdoor** - When faced with an outright refusal to budge on price or terms the Backdoor

gives your counterpart room for manoeuvre whilst saving face.

- **Name the emotion** - when you are in the conversation and you see or hear an emotion from the client, you should name that emotion.

- **Tone and quality of your voice** - Inflection at the end of a statement or a question can change the whole meaning of the words.

- **Setting the agenda** - is all about discovering what is important for them and allowing them to discover what's important for you.

Resources:

www.kahvay.com

11.Partners

If you want to go fast, go alone. If you want to go far, go together"- African proverb

There's no right or wrong answer about whether to join forces with a sales partner or make your sales on you own. If, as a vendor, you sell direct to the customer, that is great because you keep all the money. Some of the very big computer manufacturers sell direct, others work with partners. To help you make a choice about whether to work with a partner (or partners), let's examine both options.

Pros and cons

When you work alone, not only do you keep all the money and the profit, but you also have complete control of the messaging. That's all very well when you know all the potential customers in the market. But the cost of a sale is higher because it takes you longer to gain access to all those customers, and you are doing all the work, creating all the marketing, the contacts and everything else necessary. By working with a partner, you are reducing the cost of sale.

The major advantage of partners is that they are already dealing with the customers you want to talk to. They may have already introduced other products, so access is quicker if you can make that partnership work properly. And, usually, it's better to be recommended into a relationship than start a new one. In other words, partnerships can make the difference between a cold call and a warm call.

Not only that, but your partners may also find new customers for you that you haven't even thought of, giving you a much wider network of potential customers. For example, a large corporate reseller might have 3,000 software products on their books and many teams of people taking to customers every minute of every working day. Such a warm contact base and with the partner selling at your side, you could grow your own sales exponentially.

Another consideration, particularly in the software sector in the US and UK, relates to the difficulty trying to become a preferred supplier on a customer's books. Sometimes, that's just not possible. The vendor may not adhere to all the delivery mechanisms and may not therefore have the preferred supplier's status. Whereas a partner might already be on the PSL (preferred suppliers list) and have all the legal agreements in place.

No time to sit back

Having a partner doesn't negate the fact that you still need to speak to the buyer and the end user at some point, and it's best if you do that for a number of reasons:

- You get some control over that relationship – the customer may need training or handholding
- Better still, you may be able to create an opportunity for cross-selling or up-selling.

However, you must avoid trying to micro-manage your partners, because that's no way to get the best out of them. You need to have sufficient control over the customer relationship to be aware of what's going on. That way, you can feed your progress back into your business.

Accreditation

Partners might be accredited in particular areas that you, as a vendor, might not be. For instance, this can enable you to sell to governments. You may have to sign up to some partner terms and conditions that you, as the vendor, may not want to do but that may be a small price to pay if your partners have lots of customers in government. So, they may require specific Ts & Cs that then give you the opportunity to ride on the coattails of their existing agreements.

You may find a customer that needs to transact business with you, but you can't do it directly because you haven't got the prerequisite accreditations, or you can't tick the right framework boxes for them. However, a partner may already have those in place, so you can introduce the partner and they transact the business for you. This can benefit all parties because you both bring something to the table.

Risks

Working with a partner goes wrong when the relationship is unbalanced. Just like any relationship, if you treat that relationship with respect, if you value that relationship and if you put effort into the agreement, it will be a good relationship. If it's not a good relationship, it's time to walk away.

One of the biggest challenges in a good partnership is the personalities involved. You must understand and evaluate how much the relationship is worth to their business and to yours. If the relationship breaks down, the partner could 'switch sell'. A 'switch sell' occurs when you have a meeting with the customer which appears to go well, but your partner sells your competition's products rather than yours. Perhaps the partner's argument is that your competition's product is a bit cheaper. That's the absolute worst-case scenario for a 'switch sell' which, fortunately, happens very rarely. More often than not, complex transactions involve a three-way conversation between customer, partner and you (as vendor), so switch selling is less likely to occur.

Also, partners may also not follow up on leads that you give them. That's the equivalent of leaving gold on the table. You've created the campaign, you've given them some leads, and they don't follow up these leads. Or the partner could run a campaign and you don't follow up. It's up to both of you to play your part and fulfil your responsibilities.

On the other hand, a salesperson could try and bypass the partner. This is extremely bad behaviour and is the same as switch selling, but in reverse. If you've got a partner agreement in place for a particular customer, it's fine for you to talk directly to them so long as the deal ends up back with the partner.

The only exception to this rule is if the customer decides that they no longer want to work with the partner for some reason and want to negotiate directly with another partner or with you (as the vendor). After all, there should be no exclusivity, and we sometimes forget that the customer is in the driving seat. The customer is paying, so they get to choose. These situations need to be managed carefully with explicit sympathy for the partner who may have invested time and money to pursue this deal. Your vendor partner team internally should be able to advice you on how this is handled.

Selecting a partner

You may have a colleague who has specific responsibility for managing partnership relationships. If so, your first step in selecting a partner is to talk with your partnership manager. This person manages those relationships on an overall basis, and so you may get some recommendations to pursue. If, for example, your product was in the retail sector, your partnership manager might suggest that one partner had already produced some good results.

Alternatively, you might have had success with a partner you have dealt with in the past. If so, you can make your own recommendation about partnering with them. If they're not currently a partner, the partnership manager could take a look at them and give you a very swift 'yes' or 'no'.

Once you have a suggested partner, you need to develop the relationship – you (as a vendor) and a prospective partner need to get on.

Avoid having too many partners because successful relationships take time and effort. Just like a juggler, you can only keep so many plates spinning at a time, so select a partner for each area or market segment perhaps a mid-sized partner with two or three salespeople and a large partner with as many as 20. salespeople

Being top of your partner's list

Partners are interested in the quality of the leads that you bring them, and the quality of your campaigns. These are what matter most.

Ultimately, your partnership must be relevant to their customer base because, if you are not, and if the margins are thin, they are not going to try hard for you. An uphill battle is seldom attractive for them, and, like all salespeople, they will take the path of least resistance.

Partners can be precious about their contacts, and rightly so, because it's their data:

- They have worked hard to get their information, so you've got to earn the right to access it.
  Your priorities in making a success of any partnership:
- You've got to be relevant in the marketplace
- You've got to do the right amount of advertising
- You've got to be out there yourself

You cannot just say, "Create me a market." You've got to be part of that story and help create the market. Partners can, indeed, be precious about their contacts, so you've got to give them a good reason to pick up the phone on your behalf.

Make it a mandatory part of your diary every week (and no less than once a fortnight), to talk to your partners to maintain your close working relationship. Aim to find out what they're doing, see how you can help them with a new campaign, or just to keep an activity progressing and ensure that they know your product is the clear choice for their clients. They're not supposed to be the experts on your product, but they need to know enough to capture the customer's interest. If they are not comfortable with your business, they will not be able to sell you to their customer. Sufficient familiarity is essential, being enough knowledge to be a 10-minute expert.

Your job is to try and make your product more attractive than the rival product in your partner's portfolio. Make your product easier to understand and therefore easier to sell.

The long term view

"If you're going to a party, bring a bottle."- Tony Alder- Partner Director

You can't simply approach a new partner and say, "What have you got for me today?" The first step is **account mapping**. This where you meet your partner and discuss each other's area of expertise and find out where there is synergy. At this time, you can agree which customers you're each going to target and how you can run campaigns that share contacts. Account mapping also opens the possibility of targeting new market areas/clients together.

If you want to join the party, bring a bottle. So, make a contribution to the success of the relationship, even if it is a small contribution maybe a introduction to a contact. Entering a partnership by leading with an outstretched hand out is never a successful ploy and a very poor plan.

Partners have access to power

Everyone wants access to power, to the decision makers who will sign off on your product. But how are you going to get to them? You will need to take several steps to get to see the right person and, potentially, several weeks or months will elapse. But your partner may have these decision makers on speed dial because they're already talking to them

113

about a range of other different products. All your partner has to do is recommend you or invite you to give a demo at their next meeting with the customer. That's the value of partners - they have existing connections.

As your partner already has a portfolio of other products and has already done deals with various organisations, they can add credibility to what you are selling. In turn, this gives the customer confidence to hear your pitch. Make sure you've convinced the partner that you are a good business to be dealing with, because this helps the partner sell you into the customer. Even better, if your partner has similar products in their portfolio, they implicitly validate your story.

So, do you work alone or with partners? Whenever possible, work with partner because:

- They open doors,
- They add credibility,
- They give you a greater reach, even an international reach, and
- They already have the necessary accreditations, which are often laborious for you to earn, while all you need is one contract with the partner.

As an added bonus, you have the chance to enjoy the team approach to customers. In particular, you may find that working alone seldom achieves results in the public sector. Here, you need partners who already have long-term relationships with the big organisations. Working alone, you will spend your life trying to get to the right people. However, if you're propped up by a partner they know and trust and who has recommended you, then you will get a much warmer reception.

Summary
- **Pros and Cons** – alone you keep the profit, but the cost of sale is higher and could take longer
- **No time to sit back** – just because you have a partner doesn't mean you should stop talking to the customer
- **Accreditation** – ride on the coattails of your partner's existing accreditation agreements
- **Risks** – always keep the partner relationship in balance and treat it with respect
- **Selecting a partner** – don't try to keep too many plates spinning at the same time
- **Being top of your partner's list** – your job is to make your product more attractive than your rival's and therefore easier to sell.
- **Long term view** – if you're going to a party, bring a bottle
- **Access to power** – the value of partners is that they already have the connections you want

Resources
www.successfulchannels.com
www.channelweb.co.uk
www.openviewpartners.com
https://www.saleshacker.com/channel-sales-direct-sales-strategy/

12.Renewals

The lifeblood of the sales business is the strength of the renewals business.

In all cases, there is an endpoint to a current maintenance or subscription contract that needs to be faced and overcome. This is where the skill of the salesperson really gets tested.

Do you feel better about winning a new £100,000 deal or not losing a £100,000 renewal? If you felt better about winning the new deal, then you would be out of business very quickly as your base will leak, renewals don't take as much effort as new deals, but they should have equal importance to the business and to salespeople responsible for them

Why renewals are so important

Brand, new business becomes tomorrow's renewals.

Imagine your business has a total revenue of £1m and 60% of that is made up of renewals that are due each year. If you were to lose £250,000 of renewal business, you would need a pipeline of £several million, because the close rate and the cost to win most new business is significantly higher than a renewal.

To put this another way, think of your business as a bucket of water with a hole in it. A portion of that business will be renewals and a portion will be brand, new business. If you have a leaking bucket and you have a 25% hole in it, the new business you are able to pour in at the top almost never makes up for the hole at the bottom. You end-up in a deficit position. Also, it's also not a great advert for your company that, each year, a quarter of your business leaves.

Renewals represent a constant revenue stream. They allow you to invest in other things like launch new products or even invest in your sales force.

There is always the kudos and flag-waving allure of a new business win, whereas renewals are less exciting for everyone. But, as the cost of renewals is typically much lower than new business, the finance department in your organisation will always be happier if you spend more time keeping your existing clients than hunting for new ones. For all their faults, finance people recognise the importance of renewals.

The 'hunters' of new deals attract the plaudits, while the 'farmers' tending the renewals keep the business afloat. If you like, renewals are the bread and butter of the business. This is an interesting conundrum, as it's an example of emotions and news around new deal wins driving behaviour

A low renewal rate equals death If you have a low renewal rate, eventually the company will die.

If a client is willing to spend money in the first year and they decline the offer to renew in the second, surely something went horribly wrong? Well, maybe, but there are lots of reasons that may be out of the salesperson's control. So, be aware very early on that the client is unlikely to renew. Here are some examples:

- The client company has been taken over
- Leadership decision-makers related to your project have changed

- The project that funded the purchase has come to an end
- The product is failing
- The perceived value of the product is low
- There has been a lack of training or use of the product
- The budget has been tightened
- There has been a company policy change
- There has been 'competitor bleed' over your space (the client already has another product that is similar to yours and already has a larger spend with these competitors)
- There has been a failure in compliance
- The vendor has failed to offer enough attention over the life of the contract
- There has been poor support and maintenance

There are probably other reasons applicable in more specific situations - the above is simply a general list of possible reasons you may encounter.

How to maintain renewals

"Sales," so the saying goes, "is a contact sport," so why do so many companies forget about contact?

There is very little presales effort involved in renewals and there's very little travelling but staying in touch with the customer throughout the contract is essential. You must provide a service to the customer in whatever you're doing for the duration of that contract.

Keep in touch, not just to sell, but perhaps just to email them something newsworthy in their market or that a competitor has done. Ensure the users of your product are well trained, even set up Centres of Excellence for larger organisations to provide internal assistance for themselves.

The point of keeping in touch is really to make sure that the customer is happy with the product and to make sure that they renew, because renewal is predictable and easier revenue to generate.

And the way to keep customers happy is to be in touch regularly, not just in the month before the renewal date. You should approach the renewal date with time on your side:

- Do your research before calling and never discuss price of renewal on the first call
- Establish where they are with their business and what they are planning to do next.

Large deals are still human interactions (at least for the time being) and a relationship is based on two elements:

- Firstly, how does being in the presence of that person make you feel, and
- Secondly, how much time do you spend in that person's company either face-to-face or on the phone, or on the other end of an email?

If the first is positive, it's unlikely that you will upset a client. So, what really matters is the amount of contact you have with the client over the lifetime of the contract.

The absolute worst behaviour from a salesperson is selling to a client and then not contacting them at all until a month before the renewal, presenting their procurement department with a quotation to renew. How would you feel if you were the customer: ignored, unimportant and taken for granted as simply a source of money for the vendor?

Ideally, before renewal is due, you should call every month (or at least every 90 to 120 days). You don't want your customer saying, "Why didn't you tell me about that automatic renewal clause?" or "Why didn't you tell me about that 10% uplift for late renewals?" To make contact just a month before renewal or, worse, the day before renewal, looks like you are just issuing an invoice and expecting payment.

Instead, your approach might be, "I see your renewals are coming up, so I just want to check the service is working for you. Let's not talk about money right now, let's just talk about how your business. Are you planning to expand?" After all, your goal is not only to get the customer to renew but also to get them to look at their next three years. This will help them to consider whether they will they need more of your products and services to help their business achieve its goals.

This approach to renewals is about maintaining relationships, which is vitally important, particularly in the kind of remote world we all live in today.

What's a good renewal rate?

The level of a good renewal rate depends on how seriously the business takes renewals. If you simply issue invoices to clients (yes, people still do that and, at best, achieve only about a 60% renewal rate) then it's highly likely that your company will put enormous attention on new sales

As a rule of thumb, a good renewal rate in the software business is anything over 90%. 100% is rarely possible, and 75% is a troubled place to be. If you can keep non-renewals in single digits (below 10%), you've got a sustainable business. But if the rate creeps up to 15%, you've got a problem. And anything above 20% means you've got a major issue to address.

Stickiness and Value

To maintain a high renewal rate depends on how important you are to the customer. Some people call this the "stickiness" of the Product and therefore the relationship.

Some drivers of "stickiness" relate to questions such as:
• Is there plenty of competition out there for your product?
• Just how valuable are you to the customer?
• If they didn't have your product, how badly would it impact their business?
• How much is your product worth to their organisation?

Some salespeople forget that selling is a people business. You must be clear about the relationship of you (and your salespeople) to the customers? After all, we're all human beings. People buy from people. The best way to develop a good relationship is to talk and talk about what your product is able to do for the customer, it's value and its importance. If you don't keep in touch, you may be labouring under the false impression that the person who bought the product three years ago is still with the company. That person could well have left soon after the original deal was struck.

"Stickiness" sounds silly but it's actually an important concept because it relates to how easily your customer could remove your product, and so remove the obligation to pay a renewal cost. If it's difficult, the cost of change is going to be a factor that's taken into account, not just the benefits of another rival product. This is the sort of decision that is always something a chief executive is concerned about:

- "Will it mean sending my people on another training course?"
- "What is the risk of change to another service provider?"
- "Can we just put pressure on the current supplier to reduce the price?"

"Stickiness" depends on how entrenched you are with the customer and the quality of the service you have been providing during the contract period. So, concentrate on building "stickiness."

Value dies with age
When someone first starts using a new product, they're invariably excited about their great decision to buy a new car, a new laptop or a new multi-million-dollar service. They are almost selling the item themselves to everyone they meet.

But are they still so excited after 24 months, or has it just become another utility? They expect it to work and now, maybe, it doesn't look so cool because there is another model or apparently a better service available.

In reality, the value hasn't diminished. Typically, the value is the same as the day they bought it, but, for them, the value has died emotionally in their heart. They look at their neighbours or their competitors and start worrying about the need to change or upgrade.

Upselling and cross-selling
Upselling within renewals means, "I don't just want you to renew. I want you to look at a new portfolio of our products." It might be more capacity, more licences, more phones or more bandwidth than the customer has currently contracted for.

Just as you should do with a new client, upselling at renewal is a great opportunity to sell a longer period and increase the value, along with the ticket price. To succeed, try the Goldilocks method:

• Always offer three quotations to your client: quotes for one year, three years and five years are a good start.
These represent the three choices that Goldilocks faced, and these may or may not be appropriate in your business however for example You'll find that the discount takes care of itself between one year and three years (typically about 10-20%) and simply add a further discount line of 10% to the five-year quote so there is an advantage to the client for making a longer commitment, I have used this method with a number of clients over the years and it's more often than not successful.

If you send only a one-year quote to the customer, they have a binary decision: one year or nothing. However, if you send all three quotes, then the discussion is changed to: "How much is saved by moving to a longer term?"

The Goldilocks method works particularly well if you are dealing with procurement teams. They are usually targeted on making savings on every purchase, such as a particular percentage rate. Therefore, these people need to be able to show their management team just how much they have saved by going for that three-year contract. If you don't send the other quotes, they can't show that they've made a saving, and won't be rewarded or recognised. That is not in their best interest and certainly not yours.

Similarly, cross-selling is selling a different product altogether. To be successful in cross-selling, you should start a long way out from the renewal date.

As always, regular contact will help build and maintain a close relationship and pave the way for a cross-sell. For instance, try booking group meetings with all your customers collectively especially if they are in the same market segment, perhaps two or three times a year. In this way, you have created a reason to speak to each of them times a year.

You can try to get similar customers together in a room because you can cover so many bases, and they enjoy the opportunity to meet and talk with others facing similar challenges. The agenda can include renewals and cross-sell opportunities. You can also invite new customers and new prospects who haven't yet purchased. Let them all sit in a room full of customers and they will want to talk about how great their decisions have been. At meetings like these, you get instant references, and you get good feedback, which is hugely valuable for your own product and marketing teams.

If you try to upsell or cross-sell just days before a renewal, the customers have no opportunity to study the product or get finance approval All this takes time, which is why you must aim **to sell through the cycle.**

Forecasting renewals
The accuracy with which you can forecast renewals is based on the value you've brought to that business. At the end of a meeting with your existing customer talking about the renewal, you need to come away from that meeting with a likelihood (from one to ten) - are they going to renew or not and why.

At a renewal meeting, it's the same conversation you might have for a new business meeting, but customers should be more open with you about the product and what it has done for them. Does it save them time, energy, and money? In short, does it bring value to their organisation?

With all products, value diminishes over time, so you need to remind customers of that value and how much easier it has made their operation. And of course, don't forget to mention the challenges involved in changing supplier.

Summary:

- **Why renewals are so important** – they are the lifeblood of the business, representing a constant revenue stream.
- **How to maintain renewals** – stay in regular contact to build and maintain relationships.
- **What's a good renewal rate** – keep non-renewals in single digits (less than 10%).
- **Stickiness and value** – high levels of renewals depend on how important you and your product are to the customer.
- **Value dies with age** – it's all in the mind but nonetheless real.
- **Upselling and cross-selling** – like Goldilocks, offer at least three choices and give the customer time to decide.
- **Forecasting renewals** – it all depends on the value you have brought to the customer's business.

Resources:

- Books: The Expansion Sale: Four Must-Win Conversations to Keep and Grow Your Customers by Erik Peterson, Tim Riesterer

13.The Covid Effect

Finally, it is important to consider the impact of the biggest social and economic event of 2020/21 – Coronavirus (Covid 19). The most striking aspect of the pandemic from a sales and marketing perspective is that sales cycles, in certain instances, are now starting to speed up.

While earlier deals caught up at the start of Covid 19 may have been delayed, newer opportunities seem to be moving at a faster pace because working practices have changed.

Whereas before the crisis meetings would have been scheduled days, even weeks, ahead and then there would have been travel to meetings, the polite rigmarole offering of coffees, now an email invitation to a video discussion gets an immediate response. There is no travelling time involved – there is even no need to put on that smart suit and polished shoes.

The world has changed, and the pace of exchange is moving faster; you can find yourself moving rapidly from initial conversation to Terms & Conditions and Legals of a contract in a matter of weeks or even days.

As we emerged from the worst of the pandemic in late 2021 not only have things changed on the sales side, but things will also need to change on the marketing side, much more will be online, and the successful marketing and sales teams will be the ones that understand this and make necessary modifications.

14.Summary

In summary I think if you have read most or all of the chapters you will have a good grounding in what it is to sell to a large corporate entity, you will need to practice these processes and behaviours like any skill and the more you do this the more you will learn, different clients will have different needs and ways of doing things as will organisations that you work for, however I have tried to keep this generic so as to be as applicable in most situations with most companies.

You will hit the wall sometimes.

You know when you have made it in a profession when you have overcome adversity and come out smiling and winning, that's my measure of a good salesperson, not one that just wins all the time (not too sure if that person even exists over a long period of time?) success teaches us far less than failure and we only really fail completely when we stop and take note of where we are and what we are doing. I welcome the opportunity to fail on occasion and learn as it builds bedrock for the next step of evolution as a salesperson and as an individual. You will fail at some point get comfortable with that as it's a fact, that proves you tried something and by trying you learn I can't stress enough how you will need to find a way to be resilient to these setbacks, it's not how we deal with success that defines a character and a salesperson, but how we deal with failure, then get on with building success in the future. It's a practiced skill and you will learn how.

Thanks

As with a great deal of books I have had a huge amount of assistance from industry veterans, I'd like to thank them all sincerely for participating and sharing their knowledge in an altruistic way, as like me they were keen to pass on their learnings to the next generation of enterprise salespeople.

Toby Marsden- Leadership
Duncan Bradford-Presales
Camille Morgan- Partners
Ian Stimpson-Presales
Milko Van Duijl- Leadership
Steve Peters- Procurement
Nikki Horwood- Field marketing
Giles Morgan – Negotiation (www.Kahvay.com)
Tom Kennedy- Renewals
Mike Southby- Renewals

If you would like to get in touch with any of these wonderful folks to talk about your challenges, some of them are open to coaching and consulting sessions, please get in touch via sellingthenextgen@gmail.com

Reviewers:
Oz Khan, Smeeta Sinah, Richard Fish, Louise Ashbrook, Steve Orman, Lez Dwight, Will Horrell, Claire Scull, Rob Limbrey, Cameron Stephens, James Stewart, Ed Palmer, Admiral James Stavridis, Elliott Veale.

Final note

In closing I want to let you know how excited I am to think you have read my book and you are using it in your daily work as a salesperson in the enterprise space, I am also excited for you as If I had my time again I would certainly go into this line of work, it's treated me to some amazing opportunities and a huge amount of learning that I'm massively grateful for, I have interacted with thousands of unique individuals some I liked and some I didn't, but I think for a non-celebrity to be able to make that many acquaintances is a real gift, some of them are close friends too.

If you liked this book them, please send a copy on to your friends' colleagues or even your enablement team at work as this information is here to be shared and if you buy in quantity, we can arrange a discount (see, I'm always selling). If you want to ask me any questions, please email me at sellingthenextgen@gmail.com and I'll try to answer as fast as I can.

Good luck and have a good-long ride on the roller-coaster of selling it's tough, amazing, exhilarating and rewarding, just exactly how I want my life to be.

Printed in Great Britain
by Amazon

79066388R00075